The author was born
on 2nd April 1921, in a religious and
a noble family of Bengal in India and had widely
travelled.

Although he was
an Engineer by profession,
he was a potential performing artist, a
vocalist and an instrumentalist too.

But his keen
interest and vast
study in the field of philosophy
of life, human behaviour and their
psychology for more than 40 years, has
enabled him to produce a quasi technical
book, in a lucid and popular language, to boost
the morale and to solve the psychological
problems of the common man.

HOW TO BE
HAPPY, HEALTHY AND RICH

S.N. BOSE

BOOKS FOR ALL

DELHI-110052

Published by:
BOOKS FOR ALL
C-2/9, 3rd Floor,
Community Centre,
Ashok Vihar, Phase II, Delhi - 110052

Laser Typeset by:
ABC *for* DTP
6, Rajdhani Enclave, Delhi-110034.

Printed at:
Unique Color Carton
New Delhi-110064

PRINTED IN INDIA

To

My Son

Krishnendu Bose.

Preface

What do men aspire to, acquire or achieve? The answer is mostly-Wealth. By this, we generally mean money, which is instrumental in acquiring many other things in the world. To acquire riches we must have knowledge and wisdom.

But to acquire knowledge and wisdom we have to be healthy, physically and mentally.

I have tried to present to the common men and women, the simple key to all these problems. This book is written for students, service and businessmen, the middleaged and the old, whether men or women.

A line or two on why and how I was inspired to write this book.

In my childhood, I had occasion to attend religious discourses regularly and in that context to read such books that inspired my philosophical mind. By the time I reached the age of 30, I started reading books on psychology, yoga and others relating to human behaviour. Later, when I was about 45, my life took a dramatic turn when a renowned orthopedic surgeon inspired me to indulge in the science of psychotherapy. I took up the hobby seriously, and in course of time, cured as many as six patients (two of them were potential suicides). Later still, I got more and more interested in the subject and continued my pursuits.

In this small book, I have tried to place before you, some simple facts and methods by which you can try to improve your mental and physical condition, so that you achieve peace, pleasure, happiness, as well as riches.

I have generally used the word he, to cover both sexes. The case histories mentioned in the book are all real, but generally the names and places are changed for obvious reasons.

At the end, of the book is a list of books for further reading.

If, from this book you acquire poise, pleasure and plenty;

I shall have been rewarded at the age of seventy.

S. N. BOSE

Contents

Introduction

This book provides the common reader in India with a basic and adequate knowledge of physical and mental sickness, its cause, prevention and cure, in simple language.

As a writer, editor and researcher, I have found it a good companion in day-to-day life, practically useful for men and women of any age. It is also an inspiration to those seeking a knowledge of what is for our times good general human behaviour. Its kaleidoscopic treatment has impressed me. The fact, too, that it is derived from its author's own direct experience of living, makes it reliable and relevant for all of us in India today.

Jehanara Wasi

CHAPTER I

Your Body and Mind

We can see our body, but the complicated parts of it and their functions are not known to the common man. And knowledge about the mind is still vaguer and more abstract to the common man.

Primarily, our body consists of the digestive, circulatory and nervous systems and, most important, the set of glands and the prime controller of our body, the brain.

The various parts of the body and the functions of its organs, may be known from any medical textbook or a popular book on physiology, but the salient features of the body and their inter-relations will be dealt with here at some length to enable you to understand how they are affected or impaired.

Regarding the functions of the mind, these are available in any good textbook on psychology. But as you will see a little later, that this is a very important aspect; because, it controls many of our diseases. Hence, this has also been dealt with here, in slightly greater detail in popular ways.

But only to know your body and your mind will not be so useful if you do not know what diseases the body may suffer from, and how to prevent or cure them.

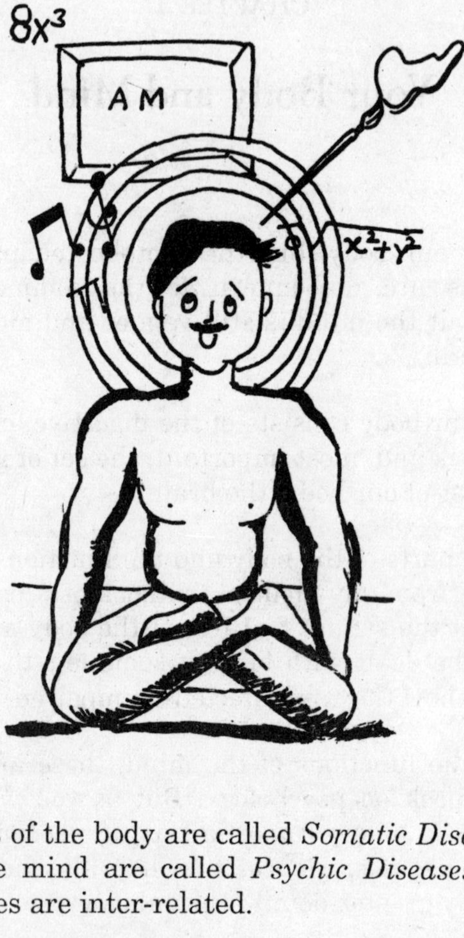

The diseases of the body are called *Somatic Diseases* and the diseases of the mind are called *Psychic Diseases*. These two types of diseases are inter-related.

So, there are Psycho-Somatic Diseases and Somato-Psychic Diseases. Psycho-Somatic Diseases are the physical diseases caused by mental imbalances and the Somato-Psychic Diseases are mental abnormalities caused by physical ailments. Psycho-Somatic Diseases creep into our body without our knowing about them and are very common.

Dr. Hans Selye of Montreal University, carried out researches during 1936 and found out how our bad emotions can cause us to be sick. Most people who go to the doctor do not know that their illnesses are due to their mental attitudes. But it is difficult to convince them that most of them have not learnt how to live and love and so continue collecting bad emotions and ultimately become a prey to diseases. These bad emotions stimulate the autonomous nervous system and ultimately produce *Emotionally Induced Illness* (E.I.I.) in us.

Now, how do we control these illnesses? *Pituitary*, the master gland, also called the conductor of the *Endocrine Orchestra*, (that is only about the size of a pea), lies in the small hollow in the skull just behind the top of the nose, and is attached by a thin stalk to the *Hypothalamus* almost at the base of the brain. This pea-size miraculous gland has three lobes. Many of the hormones produced by the front lobe affect the working of other ductless endocrine glands like, *Thyroid, Adrenal* and *Gonads*.

The *Thyroid* is mostly involved in the body's *Metabolism*. The *Adrenal* is a pair of glands at the top of the kidneys, which secretes *Adrenalin* and *Cortisone*. The hormone adrenalin passes on to the blood stream, which is prepared to face emergency action, such as flight and fight.

Now, you see that the pituitary gland is responsible for controlling our emotions. The pituitary has many other functions also.

Our Emotions, Good and Bad

While we live, we face emotional bombardment with good and bad emotions. But the pity is that the good emotions (superficial emotions) generally are only skindeep and can be perceived by others from our features and outward behaviour. The bad emotions (fundamental emotions) are such that they percolate into and excite our endocrine glands and make us sick. The pity is that the life span of these fundamental emotions is long, and may continue till the later part of our lives. If you don't take care of it at an early stage of your life, it will take a grip on you, and may continue throughout your life.

Now, if both your physical and mental spheres are affected, what is left of you, to work with, and enjoy life?

We have to protect both our body and mind from falling a victim to disease. There are several ways to do this. Let us examine the seriousness of the bad emotions first. Bad emotions produce stresses. The pituitary reacts to a vast variety of stresses, which also promote bacterial and viral infections by releasing hormones. There are other stresses also which activate in controlling the body temperature, moisture, muscular exhaustion, drug effects and injuries. Dr. Selye found (1936) that the greatest stresses are the psychic stresses. Unpleasant emotions, which when acute, produce many hormones, and have a profound effect on us. It may last for a longer period of life than the stresses due to infection, which generally do not last for more than a few weeks.

The Somatotrophic Hormone (S.T.H.) and the Adrenocorticotrophic Hormones (A.C.T.H.).

We have referred earlier to the pituitary gland which when activated, produces various hormones, one which mobilises the body's defences is called the *Somatotrophic Hormone* (S.T.H.). This works against infections. But the S.T.H. also produces symptoms of "Being Sick". Dr. Selye showed that the same feeling is perceived by us if we are infected by some virus or bacteria. By administering *Adrenocorticotrophic Hormones* (A.C.T.H.) intravenously, the effect of S.T.H. is cancelled and the feeling of "being sick" is minimised or removed, whether or not the actual infection has been removed from the body. The A.C.T.H. (which the pituitary coaxes the adrenals to produce), can work miracles by the release of Cortisone. But the prolonged use of A.C.T.H. can be bad for us and have an adverse effect, that is the A.C.T.H. stress diseases may follow. A few examples are impaired resistance to infection, pneumonia, asthma, tuberculosis, peptic ulcer, irritable colon, gall bladder-like pain, emotional appendicitis, flatulence, belching, headache, neurodermatitis, backache and many other ailments.

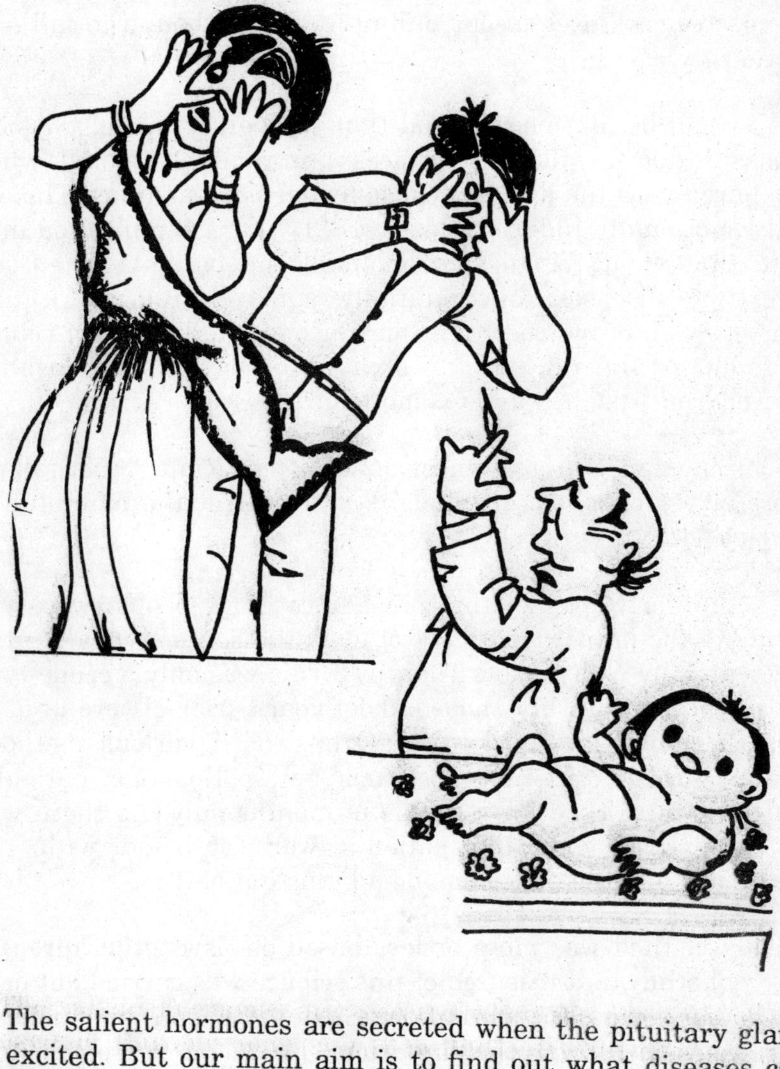

The salient hormones are secreted when the pituitary gland is excited. But our main aim is to find out what diseases can creep into our body, that are not due to virus or bacterial infection or to malfunctioning of any organ, but are due to the unusual conditioning of the body or congenital defects or deformities, and how they can be prevented or cured.

If we disturb our biological clock, or torture our body to the extreme limit of our endurance or do not eat those foods adequately, which are beneficial for our body, or eat those foods to excess that are detrimental to our body's health, or do not use correct postures in our daily life, we are bound to fall sick physically.

You will be alarmed to read that the percentage of physical diseases due to all these causes are relatively small when compared with the diseases cause by our bad emotions. This we call Emotionally Induced Illness (E.I.I.). For example, you may note that about 70 to 75 percent of the patients of gastro-intestinal diseases, have initially suffered from E.I.I. and almost 80 to 85 percent of all headaches are due to E.I.I. only and about 30 percent of skin diseases are because of neurodermatitis, i.e., due to emotional stresses.

The layman and even most general physicians (G.P.), place more stress on physical ailments and neglect the mental side altogether.

In the early part of this present century, people were not aware of the proper treatment of mental diseases. They used to be treated by 'Substitutes Therapy". This was only a crude type of 'psychotherapy'. For thousands of years, people were used to this therapy. The quacks and 'Ozhas' used various methods and prescribed different nostrums and potions for patients, which often worked for a couple of months only. As there was no other way out, the patients were satisfied with the treatment and the quacks made a living out of it.

This method was more or less based on psychotherapy. But the real study and research of this science was carried out only in the early part of this century. Sigmund Freud, an Austrian physician (1910), for the first time, looked at it from a new angle. He found that if our psychic development is taken care of at a very early stage of life, we might emerge as individuals with balanced emotions. If our emotions were taken care of, we might then, have less E.I.I. and hence 60 to 80 percent of psychosomatic diseases could be prevented.

What Education Do We Need?

Our main aim is to have respite from E.I.I. The basic principle is the same for all, child or adolescent, young, unmarried or married, middle-aged or old. But for the different stages and sex the details of the application will be slightly different.

Everybody has to have 'Emotional Statis' and hence we have to abide by the norms of life.

We must be educated well enough, to carry on with our work. By this, I don't just mean university education. Let us see what we mean by it.

(a) It is necessary that you should be able to earn your living and hold your head above the crowd. For this, education is necessary, whether university education, or craftsmanship, or farming, or anything that suits you.

(b) But at the same time, you have to cultivate good and healthy emotions and eliminate bad and unhealthy emotions. This is absolutely essential.

The second proposition is more essential than the first. Without good and healthy emotions you cannot have emotional statis. And if, you develop E.I.I., you will not be able to carry on with your formal education; and even if you are able to get an education, it will be pretty difficult to get along in this tough world, the more so if you remain sick all the time, physically or mentally.

To keep the body fit, you have to know first the different parts of the body and their functions. Dr.A.A. Michele has stressed the right posture while we are still or moving. This will save us from many of our body aches. Your muscles are attached to several bones and you yourself can discover that one muscle, if improperly balanced, can upset the functioning of the other muscles. There are a few very good exercises in yoga to illustrate this. These are *Mulabandha, Mahamudra* and *Mahabandha*. Our spinal chord spreads from the root of the brain to near the anus. Spiritual or psychic energy is said to lie in the lower abdomen region. Dr. Vansant G. Rele, who has made an extensive study of the subject, says that the '*Shusumna Nadi*' through which the 'Serpent Power' travels, is probably one of the Cranial nerves, of which there are eleven pairs. At the base of the skull, the vagus nerve endings are called the 'Ganglion'. Gradually, the nerves travel down the spinal column through the neck, chest, abdomen and then end in, and are connected to the Solar Plex (Kundalini Charka) at the lower abdomen. The vagus also has filamental connections with the renal, hepatic, splenic and pancreatic plexes. Vagus is the nerve which is composed of sensory and motor fibres (both outgoing and incoming).

In all three Mudras, that is the Mahabandha Mudra, Mulabandha Mudra and Maha Mudra, one thing is common. That is, to carry out these Mudras, we have to contract the anus muscles with the naval lower abdomen and the trunk.

Those who have practised these Mudras correctly have been free from many shortcomings of the organs situated at the lower portion of the trunk.

The spiritual or psychic energy is said to lie in the lower abdomen region. Hence, it is important that we practise those yoga exercises that will energise these regions. It has been found that the yogis (Sages) knew these Cerebro-spinal and automatic nervous systems as far back as 200 B.C. The nervous system consisted of a delicate network of 72,000 nadis (nerve). The yogis also discovered that nervous maladies are caused by fear, hate, anxiety and other emotions and stresses. These could be cured or alleviated by "Pranayama" Asans and clear thinking. Hence, know once and for all that the mind is far more important than your body, which is conditioned by the mind.

Education to Train Our Mind

A little while ago we pleaded for a proper education, so that we could hold our heads up and live a pleasant life. But what is the type of education, we should have and why?

The education and care of the body and mind starts from the cradle or to be more precise, from the mother's womb. So, the mother's proper physical and mental health is an absolute must. Though the father's contribution to the development of the baby cannot be ignored, the mother's role is supreme even before the actual birth of the child.

Then, when the child is born, for the first couple of years, the mother's love, affection and guidance provide a good momentum for its development, till the father takes over partially. The period, till the child goes to school, is crucial, as the behaviour of the parents towards the child, as well as to the others, makes a permanent impression on the child's mind.

With these impressions, the child enters a new world, faces new environments, is exposed to the world outside, and has an opportunity to learn discipline, cooperation and sacrifice. Above all, he realises that he is not the final authority, that dictates his own fate. Gradually, when the boy completes his basic education, he enters the hard core practical life; he meets the opposite sex, older and younger, good and bad people and faces all sorts of odd circumstances; and is confronted by various problems.

If he could have stored some basic good emotions before coming into the world, with a slight positive effort he could enhance his emotional statis, even if he has to face the vicissitudes of life. Generally after a certain age and basic education people get married and have children. For biological as well as psychological reasons, girls should not give birth to a child after the age of 30 or 35. For boys, the age is about 35 to 40, to give birth to healthy children; that is not only physically healthy babies, but children who will grow in a healthier atmosphere too, before the parents psychology undergoes a change for the worse which may affect the healthy upbringing of children.

According to Sigmund Freud, "the child is father of man", and sex plays a very important part in developing the child into a healthy man or woman. In early childhood the child should be gradually but carefully guided to develop himself, taking care that before the environmental effects of modern living make a scar on his mind, he should be allowed to develop his natural potentiality, so that he progresses in life without being affected by the tensions of the modern world. Otherwise, he will develop anxieties and frustrations and will have stored up bad emotions. Moreover, he should be trained to lead a simple life, and not depend on artificial and flamboyant living.

Everyone needs a change from time to time for recreation, to have respite from the monotony of life. But if, he is already leading an extravagant life, then for a change, he might try to indulge in a more extravagant life, and there is no end to this.

On the other hand, if he leads a simple life and feels simple in his mind too, any type of change will reduce his drudgery and may give him pleasure.

Julian Huxley once said: "When I got bogged down by the tumult and bustle of life and was perturbed by overwork and tension, I longed for a change and recreation. Then whenever, I used to go to the seashore, look at the vast water or allow the sand particles to trickle down my fingers, the glitter of the sand particles in the setting sun, used to give me enormous pleasure and joy so as to gain energy to start my work again with full enthusiasm and vigour."

Moreover, if the child is groomed in love, that is, parents' love, love from the school, love from his closest friends; he will have opportunity enough to develop his natural instinct of love. He should be made to understand that the doctrine of love is a 'Oneway' street. He should love without expecting any return. This is the only 'true love'. Love is twice blessed, blessing him who gives and him who takes.

CHAPTER II

Emotions—How Do They Affect Us

In the previous chapter, you saw that whenever we are worried, anxious or apprehensive, those emotions change our attitude towards our work, and our lifestyle is changed. These emotions also affect our physical health for a short while.

A middle-aged couple, Mr. and Mrs. Batra were living happily in Delhi. Their son was studying at Dehradun and their daughter at Delhi. One Sunday morning when they were preparing for a picnic locally, they received the news that their son had met with a road accident and was in hospital. The father could not bear the shock and was violently sick. The wife suspected food poisoning in the breakfast she prepared, and felt guilty about it. Eventually both had to visit the nearest medical clinic.

This was a simple case of "being sick", as a result of an emotionally induced illness. This is a type of 'Reactive Depression'. The most common form of melancholic illness is reactive depression. The victims of reactive depression are generally those affected by depression, caused by Environmental Stimuli. Environmental means agents other than his own mind. This may be due to a calamity in the family or society, or due to his own illness which he does not resolve or a lack of faith in the source of help available. These can be made over, if the person affected is mature or has been given "counselling" or "positive assurances" of a solution. This can be done by a psychiatrist or a doctor. To get a psychiatrist in time is not only difficult but costly too and time consuming as well. If the attack is mild it can be tackled by the patient himself, if he is groomed for it. This will be dealt with, in a later chapter on 'self-analysis' and 'self-hypnosis.'

Primary Endogenous Depression

What the common man knows as melancholia is also called manic depression or psychotic depression. If the source of depression is internal, that is, a bio-chemical upset of the brain function and not due to any outside influence, it may be termed Primary Endogenous Depression (P.E.D.). In this disease the mood swings are often observed in patients. Aretaeus, a doctor at Alexandria in Greece, observed these symptoms in patients, sometime in the second century A.D.

Primary Endogenous Depression (P.E.D.) occurs when the chemical process in the brain (neuro-transmitters) get upset, and the passage of messages along the nerve fibres are consequently distorted. If the process activates an excess, the patient gets elated, if the activities are diminished, the patient gets depressed. This "mood swing" is rather dangerous. One does not know the real man and to deal with him is difficult.

The happy and elated condition of this maniac can be rapidly controlled by drugs. But by understanding and counselling, elation has also been controlled in many cases. I have said that the mood swing is dangerous, because it seems to have appeared suddenly for no apparent reason. Very often, the victims are from the cream of society, clever and hardworking people. The patient cannot stop talking and becomes angry and even violent, if crossed. Sometimes he is full of fanciful ideas and often embarrasses his company by curious jokes. This is the stage when someone is in an elated or maniac condition.

A young intelligent engineer in South Delhi suddenly developed the idea that he was the incarnation of a certain religious guru, and expected people to listen to his discourses and beg him for mercy. He persuaded the public to gather at his place in thousands for this purpose. His friends and relatives tried counselling, and finally psychiatrists were called in for counselling. This failed, Neorologists were then called in and he was put in a hospital and his condition monitored: 'Litheum therapy' was tried to bring the boy under control.

In the depressed condition the patient always looks on the gloomy side of life. His thinking is generally irrational; he does not respond to counselling, nor does he react to any change of environment outside his home. This P.E.D. does not generally last for more than ten or twelve months, if handled carefully and in time by a competent psychiatrist.

I had an R.D. patient with me. He was married recently and shortly after his father died. A son was born to him, but died. After these two calamities, he suffered from depression. I tried to bring him round by counselling him. But it did not work. To change the environment, was not possible. I tried two other methods. One was Work therapy and the other was Substitution therapy, to imbibe zest and pleasure in his life, so that he could recover from the thought of suicide. He was an able draughtsman, and I tried to teach him novel methods of mechanical drawing, and showed him how to achieve flawless drawings. He was so engrossed in this activity, that while at his work he almost forgot his agony. But he dreaded entering his house, where two deaths had occurred. He could not bear to face his wife and old mother and had a guilty feeling that he was the cause of the two previous calamities.

He had a teenaged sister-in-law at home whom he hardly looked at. I told him to take an interest in his sister-in-law, and to listen to radio programmes. At first he thought I was joking. I told him to try out my advice for a month and report to me. Gradually, his face and attitude both changed. At this stage, I started counselling him. Then, after about eleven months, he came to me to thank me for saving his life.

Secondary Endogenous Depression

We have seen earlier that the reactive depressions which develop as a result of environmental disorders are generally not prolonged for more than a few hours. But if it is of a profound order, then it may last for a week, or in some cases for months. Often, it is seen, that the cause of the depression in naturally avoided or relieved by counselling.

But, if the depression is not taken care of, or the cause of depression is not eluded naturally or relieved by the method of substitution, then in course of time, it may take another shape of depression. This is called Secondary Endogenous Depression (S.E.D.). Though this Secondary Endogenous Depression (S.E.D.) is also an offshoot of Reactive Depression (R.D.), it is to be borne in mind that R.D. can possibly be cured by Counselling or some environmental change. But the S.E.D. can be treated by physical methods only (drugs or medicines). The physical methods are not advocated, unless it becomes absolutely necessary. This will be dealt with in Chapter VII.

Symptomatic Depression

If an individual is strained physically or mentally for a long time, it can cause a depression which is called "Symptomatic Depression" (S.D.). These symptomatic depression are more profound and of a deep acting nature, but are very rare when compared with the reactive depression. If the S.Ds. are allowed to remain, they might afflict the patient for years and perhaps ruin the rest of his life.

But to get rid of this S.D., one should know the cause of the source of this depression. Then you are to know the method for its treatment also.

This S.D. may be caused by prolonged addiction to drugs, alcohol or even cigarette smoking. It may also be due to malnutrition or deficiency of Vitamin 'B' or even hormone imbalance in the body.

Natural hormone imbalance generally occurs twice in a man's life; once at puberty and again at the age of 60 or 70, when the pattern of sexual activities are changed. If you consult a doctor before these crucial periods, then he will prescribe some mild hormones or suggest some altered food habits, with a larger intake of vitamins.

Women undergo such change of hormones, generally once every month just before menstruation, or after each child birth, or at the menopause. In all three cases, timely and proper care taken by a medical professional can save the patient from falling a victim to depression at these times. In women, other factors like drugs, alcohol or cigarette smoking, though rarer than men, can also be tackled by a professional expert, if taken care of in time. If such patients are left to their own devices, they may commit suicide.

Sabu Bose of Calcutta, I know, was a drug addict from his early youth. There used to be no week when he was not forced to take morphine injections to relieve his agony and uneasiness. Gradually, he changed over to heavy cigarette smoking which reached its peak to about 50 cigarettes a day.

This ultimately gave him digestive trouble and also changed his behavioural pattern and attitude. He became a maniac, a sadist and an egoistic man. He neither tried himself nor allowed any professional to interfere in these matters or to tackle these problems. He is steeped in melancholia.

CHAPTER III

Psychosomatic and Somatopsychic Diseases

It is better to have low intelligence and good emotions than to have high intelligence and bad emotions.

To earn your livelihood and raise your head high in society, you have to have good physical and mental health.

It was discussed in the previous chapters, how to keep good physical health by having a balanced diet at right intervals, practising good postures and by scientific physical exercises. Once you have the intention, it is not very difficult to carry them out. But another contributing factor to your good physical health is your good emotions. To achieve optimal hormone balance in your body, you are to stimulate your mind with pleasant and cheerful group of emotions. The medicinal value of the good emotions cannot be over stressed.

To have good mental emotions, there are various sources from which you may acquire them, viz.:-

(a) Parents.

(b) Educational Institutions.

(c) Your Work Place.

(d) Friends and Relatives.

(e) Good Books and Religious Institutions.

(a) Regarding the influence of the parents, we have already discussed it in the earlier chapter. Parents, and specially the mother, is the main source for the child, to gather momentum, regarding the touch of love. Love, the four letter miraculous word can change the whole world (including yourself).

(b) Educational institutions have great potentiality in forming the character and imparting good emotions and maturity. Our educational institutions should inculcate compulsory courses like yoga, military discipline and balanced ecology. Yoga can lead us to the way of physical, moral and spiritual health. The essence of yoga is dhyana or concentration. Concentration comes from meditation and without meditation the knowledge of the self cannot be acquired. The Stages are Dharana, Dhyana and Samadhi. Dharana is the start of concentration. As soon as Dharana is mastered, it deepens into Dhyana, the second stage of concentration, which opens the door to Samadhi, the third and highest '*Antarangas of Raj-Yoga*'. It is the absolute agreement and coordination of all the contents of the mind with regard to the object and subject contemplated, after which no more thought about it is possible. When investigation and reasoning end, there is a period of contemplation, and enlightenment finally comes to one. This leads to self-knowledge, the consciousness or unconsciousness of itself. It may take decades, or all your life, and you may never achieve Samadhi. But progress towards it is a great step, to reach this state of superconscious awareness in lives on earth.

The next step to gather good healthy emotions, is by learning military discipline. Generally we want only to order, but do not want to learn how to obey. If you do not know how to obey, how do you expect that the world will obey your order? Military personnel are trained to become 'He-Man' first. They are well trained not to be unruly and to mould "self" to discipline, so that they can judge and adjust the 'self' to a particular situation. This is for the benefit of the job at hand and not for any selfish motive.

Thirdly, training for ecology teaches personnel how to love and live, and also let others live, be they men, animals or objects of nature.

(c) Your Work Place

Men or animals cannot live by themselves. Man either works with other men, machines or objects of nature. In all these aspects, there is always a game of give and take. If you want to take, you will have to give first. As a matter of fact, it is the law of nature, that if you go on giving, nature will have to give you back today or tomorrow in some form or other to complete the cycle of evolution. The supreme way to give and dedicate is to love. If you love a person, you cannot afford to harm him anyway. You will always try to be generous and give maximum comfort and pleasure to him. As a result, you will also regain good healthy emotions which will keep you mentally cheerful and free from worries and anxieties.

(d) Friends and Relatives

True friends are rarely to be found "A friend in need, is a friend indeed." It is an art to choose a friend who shares your interests and is on the same wave length. Keep a small circle of true and intimate friends so that they not only help you in times of need but also give you good healthy emotions. It is not practical to love everybody, nor is it necessary to hate people.

I knew a 16-year-old girl, Mamata, who told me: "I hate everybody." She believed that she practised what she said. She was not aware that healthy love crept into herself. She actually loved to study subjects like mathematics and physics as well as culture Western music. I cashed in on those weaknesses and encouraged her to develop these. I was able to mould her to a great extent. Though it took quite a few years to curb her.

There is a saying in Sanskrit that good men have a number of friends. It means that "If you are generous, the whole world will be your friends."

Relatives are only relatives. They are seldom true friends. Except for a few relatives, the rest are always out to take advantage of your generosity or your weaknesses and try to grab your precious belongings.

(e) Good Books and other Religious Institutions

We have observed that a true friend is difficult to choose. But "books are very good friends", that you can choose with less efforts. Unlike friends, books are deaf. They don't get excited or react to your feelings and comments. You select a good book, read it, digest it and enjoy it. There is one drawback in books. Friends, relatives and books can also lead you astray. If you cannot select a good book, you may be ruined. Bad books and bad pictures or bad movies can be your enemy, instead of being a friend to you, if you cannot judge and make the right choice. Hence, even to be able to select a good medium of learning, you have to have some basic initial training to reach that stage.

I had a friend, N.P. Saxena, working in the same trade as mine. He always used to envy my knowledge and poise and wondered how and when I got time to read and develop such knowledge and emotional statis? I told him, "I have made it a habit to read for about fifteen minutes before I retire at night, for six days a week, which works out to nearly 70 to 80 hours a year. However busy I am, I make it a point to take a nice sleeping cap with a small dose of fifteen minutes of reading. That helps me to keep up my equity and emotional statis as well as enables me to enrich my knowledge."

Everybody should, from childhood, read religious books as well as be associated regularly with persons who have Cosmic Consciousness. When we are born, we are pure and simple. But as and when we grow up, we are prone to vices. Just to enable us to prevent us and protect ourselves from this catastrophe it is imperative that we should always be on the look out for good emotions and try to elevate our moral level.

Fundamental and Superficial Emotions

We have always two layers of emotions within us - superficial and fundamental.

Superficial emotions will be revealed from your personality and your disposition. Either you will look cheerful or morose, and act in such a manner as to reveal those attitudes. People coming into contact with you, will be able to gauge your mental condition from your attitudes and take suitable steps to match them. But the fundamental emotions are deep rooted and those apprehensions will tighten your muscles and over stimulate your endocrine glands. If these emotions are not taken care of, then in the beginning, there will be a feeling of "being sick" and later on various functional diseases may creep into your Soma or the body. This is called a psychosomatic disease.

But, it is not necessary that all the fundamental emotions produce symptoms of disease and ultimately culminate in functional diseases.

There are also good healthy fundamental emotions which give a lifetime's happiness. These are acquired by those who learned to maintain emotions of equanimity, resignation, courage, determination and cheerfulness. This is a sort of contagious disease. Persons coming into contact with such people will also gradually acquire these potentialities.

How your Mental Illness Produces Physical Illness

We have seen earlier that due to the unbalancing of your mental equilibrium your muscles become tense and the first reaction will be some aches, pains and cramps in various parts of your body. Generally, either there will be 'pain in the neck' or a feeling of "lump in the throat" (due to tightness of the muscles at the upper end of the oesophagus). And if the intensity is great, and the tightness trickles down the oesophagus then it will be difficult for you to swallow.

Statistics in two hospitals in U.S.A. in 1951 revealed that about 75 percent of the patients reporting for gastro-intestinal diseases suffered from Emotionally Induced Illness (E.I.I.).

The Stomach is one of the easy victims of emotions. Suppose you are sitting at the dinner table and are about to eat your favourite dish, and there is a ring at the door giving you very bad news, you will suddenly lose your appetite. People who generally lead such a life which gives uncertain apprehensions and tensions, develop bad appetite and often complain, either about pain in the stomach or indigestion or acidity. This has a chain reaction.

These types of bad emotions, if repeated, may lead to various functional disease such as:-

(a) Stomach Ulcer.

(b) Fibrositis.

(c) Rheumatism.

(d) Arthritis.

(e) High Blood Pressure.

(f) Diabetes.

(g) Migraine.

(h) Asthma.

Colon Affiliated Illnesses

The 28 feet intestine consists of the small intestine, and the later part of 4.1/2 feet is called the Colon. This later part, colon, is the seat of most of the emotionally induced illnesses next to the stomach, in the entire digestive system.

After the appendix, the colon ascends in your body, from the right side of the belly, then travels horizontally and ultimately descends and joins the anus as rectum. Near the right lower side of the colon, lies the appendix and near the right upper part there is the gall bladder and the liver. Due to emotions, like love, hate, fear and anxiety, the normal functions of the digestive system are disturbed. This gives a feeling of 'gas', 'belching' and 'pain' generally at the right side of the belly. And, when the intensity of emotion is grave, you get a feeling of 'bloating' and 'choking' in the oesophagus (gullet). If the emotional feeling trickles further down and is more severe, then you start 'belching'. Very often people who have to address a large gathering or are cornered by somebody who does not find a way to escape (mentally) suffer from belching that will not stop.

Near the lower end of the colon, lies the appendix and if the spasms have reached that part, there may be a feeling of 'appendix pain'.

My father was a high diabetic patient. During the summer vacation from my Engineering College, the whole family went to Shimla for a change. I being the only son, he was always worrying about me in addition to his bad health. One day from early in the morning a pain near his appendix troubled him so much that I had to summon a couple of doctors that morning for advice. They all advised immediate removal of the appendix. I, then, went to the Civil Hospital and persuaded a European Civil Surgeon to examine my father. He diagnosed the origin of the pain to be the colon and adjoining muscles and not the appendix. My father took some tablets and an adequate quantity of boiled green gourd (*louki*) which cured him.

If the spasms are in the upper right side of the colon, due to your bad emotions, then the nearest suspect would be the gall bladder. Most of the doctors would suspect it as a gall Stone or a constriction in the bile duct.

This is what happened to my wife. After giving birth to her second child, she constantly apprehended danger for the boy. As she already had some trouble regarding the health of her first son, she had all sort of apprehensions. At the age of 38 in

1964, only 3 years after the birth of her second son, she developed occasional pain near the gall bladder. Doctors prescribed palliatives for years and ultimately when the X-Rays could not reveal any defect in the gall bladder before and after the treatments, then she was convinced that her gall bladder and the bile duct were safe. She was given counselling and placebos which brought the situation under control.

Dr. Andrew C. Ivy, a Chicago physiologist, proved that emotional spasm of the small sphincter muscle at the bile duct outset can produce a pain as severe as any gall bladder attack.

Dr Schindler of U.S.A. had a similar patient. The widow had a pain in the upper right belly which was considered a gall bladder attack. On two occasions of the attack the intensity of pain was controlled by administering several doses of hypos. But after the third attack when she received a note from her son that he had moved to the war front, she had to be taken to the hospital for severe pain. But the X-Rays did not reveal any gall stone. Seeing the severity of the pain, the gall bladder was removed and the pain did not reappear for several months. The doctor was perplexed when the fourth and fifth attacks followed even after the gall bladder was removed. Then, ultimately, when the boy returned home, safe and sound, her gall bladder pain vanished for ever. This is a case of her bad emotions. You may call it Emotionally Induced Illness (E.I.I.).

These are three examples of Emotionally Induced Illness (E.I.I.) of 'being sick' near the colon. Now, if the pain develops on the left side of the colon, then there are fewer chances of the 'being sick' feeling and apprehension of some organic ailment, as there are a limited number of organs on that side of the colon. Probably, that is why, it is recommended by yogis to lie on the left side while retiring at night.

Migraine and Blood Vessels of the Skull

Women get migraine more often than men and are more sensitive to various situations than their male counterparts. When we are involved in some emotion, the capillaries in the region of the skull get flooded with blood and an undue pressure is developed in both the inside and outside the skull. When these vessels contract, headaches develop. But the severe type of headache which is called migraine, generally develops on a particular side of the skull. Only experts can find the emotional cause of migraine. There are palliatives in allopathic treatment but this can be controlled effectively with the help of homoeopathic medicines. Efforts must, however, be made to analyse and find the cause of the emotional disturbance and if it can be nullified, then gradually the migraine also vanishes.

I had a patient, Mrs. Ghose, an elderly lady, whose husband was almost bedridden for a number of years. She used to get an attack of migraine on the left side of the skull almost every 10 to 15 days. She stayed in town for two months and was under my homoeopathic treatment. During that treatment and a couple of months later, she did not have a further attack.

About 85 percent of all headaches are emotionally induced. The rest may be due to indigestion or constipation, over exhaustion, exposure to the afternoon sun (more ultraviolate rays!), defective sleeping posture and many others, which can easily be taken care of.

Neurodermatitis

Nearly 30 percent of skin troubles are emotionally induced and are called neurodermatitis. An average man has about 17 square feet of skin on his body. Basically, there are two layers of skin - epidermis and dermis. Epidermis is the tough outer layer of the skin (but comparatively thinner than the dermis), consisting of dead cells that are constantly being shed. The underlying part, epidermis is made up of rapidly dividing cells. These are continually pushing upwards and replacing the dead cells above them. Below this layer is the dermis which contains tiny blood vessels and nerve endings. There are also sweat glands and oil glands. Dermis is the real layer of the skin and it is thinnest on the lips and thickest on the scalp, palms and soles.

Let us see how an emotion can harm your skin. At every emotional manifestation, the small blood vessels squeeze down and a small amount of serum is extruded through the thin layer of the vessel. By this continual process, an appreciable amount of serum accumulates in the tissue of the dermis. Initially, the skin gets brown, then red and ultimately when enough serum is accumulated, the pressure forces its way up, to the surface and there comes the weeping, scaling, crushing and itching; a full blown case of neurodermatitis.

An old man had not had an attack of dermatitis throughout his life, till he was 68. When his first wife died, he married for the second time, a lady of the same age and within a few months, he developed dermatitis. It was seen later, that whenever he lived separately due to business or family circumstances, his neurodermatitis vanished. On investigation it was found that the domineering and dominating nature of his wife was the cause of his dermatitis. Later, this neurodermatitis was controlled by counselling his wife.

The cause of skin diseases may be many, but neurodermatitis can be controlled if the emotional statis is maintained.

Skeletal Muscles and Fibrositis

Emotion tightens the muscles, but if the intensity or duration of the emotion is greater, then we develop muscular rheumatism or fibrositis. It is not only the emotion which is important, but it is the type of emotion that is more important. The emotion developed when we are called upon to do something, we generally would not do, tells upon us and we become a victim of diseases like rheumatism, fibrositis or arthritis.

I know a landlady who was trying hard to evict her tenant, but the tenant persisted in living in the same house for several years. Fighting with the tenant, and yet allowing him to live in the same house, was too much for her. She was otherwise healthy and had not crossed 50, but because of the problematic tenant, she suddenly developed arthritis.

Maturity and Emotional Statis

This case was more of Emotionally Induced Illness (E.I.I.) than ageing. The chemical changes that went on in her body for her bad emotions all these years, constantly told upon her health.

It has been found that women fall a victim of circumstances more often than men. It is generally very difficult for them to adjust to any new situation. There are lots of people who are chronically dissatisfied all their lives. They are aggressively resentful, quick to be upset, quick to be hurt, long to hold a grudge, always struggling to change something or somebody the way they want. The result is that they are victims of ACTH stress diseases (as discussed earlier).

Let us see how the 'being sick' feeling is produced in our body and how to avoid or get rid of it at all.

In the old days, we used to think that the 'being sick' feeling was due to the effect of bacteria or virus. But it has been established that whenever our body meets the threatening conditions of fights and flights the pituitary gland is activated and as many as 12 hormones are produced. The common causes are, due to the bacterial or viral infection, exposure to heat and cold, moisture, dryness or high altitudes, muscular over exhaustion, starvation and many others. But the most important stress of all is that of the stressing emotions, which generally surpass other physical stresses in degree and duration. But, it is to be noted that the emotional stresses may produce the same effects as any other types of stresses and we get a feeling of 'being sick'. The 'infection', stresses the pituitary gland to over produce *Somatotrophic Hormones* (S.T.H.) to combat the bacteria or virus. But the emotions of defeat, futility and discouragement have exactly the same action. The immediate effects of S.T.H. are tiredness, general aching, nausea, weakness as well as the inflammations for defence against the bacteria. Mild emotional stresses repeated at intervals for a long time are more dangerous which produce a variety of conditions like, asthma, rheumatoid arthritis, high blood pressure, nephrosclerosis, periateritis, lupus and erythematosis.

Once you are a victim of all these ailments owing to emotional stress, you need some relief. The doctors may prescribe some ACTH base medicines. But as long as the ACTH medicines are continued, the disease will be under control, but no sooner is it withdrawn, the disease will reappear again, unless other methods are adopted for their cure. The type of emotions that stimulate ACTH are the agressively unpleasant emotions one gets by driving onself relentlessly towards a goal like an ambitious executive, reformer or the militant dissatisfaction of one's own self. And in return, what you get is either a peptic ulcer, arthritis or probably you may contact tuberculosis or cirrhosis of the liver due to over production of ACTH. Ultimately, you lose all the resistance needed to cure the diseases.

Apprehension and superstition probably play an important role in the development of mental aberrations.

Sampa at Calcutta, a girl of 22, I know, was appearing for her Master of Science Degree Examinations in physiology. She was intelligent and studious. But her nervousness was to play havoc in her examinations. She had a pad on which she used to keep the answer papers and write in the examination hall. She had a feeling that she faired well in all the previous examinations because of the writing board. Before the examination, she went all the way to her parents, to her country home, to fetch the pad. But she came back empty-handed as the pad was missing from the place where she previously used to keep it. Two days before the examination she wept bitterly and said that she would definitely fail. I found no other way but to resort to counselling. She was assured that pad or no pad, as she had prepared for the examination, she would get through with flying colours. For the next two days, I had to work hard on the poor girl. She made another attempt, appeared for the examination and thank God, took a first division.

This reactive type of depression was based on some fancy. If you are obsessed with a person or object, this can ultimately harm you. If you don't attain that object or do not benefit from a person, you will certainly get depressed. You have to be able to differentiate between fancy and fact. This reactive type of depression, does not last for more than a few days or weeks, but if this is not taken care of in time, either by his own will-power or through an agent, then this type of depression may produce Emotionally Induced Illness (E.I.I.).

Superficial emotion can be recognised from the patient's physical appearance and behaviour. So is the physical illness which can be recognised by a friend or relative and the patient can be described as a sick person. But if a person is sick because of fundamental emotions, then it is very difficult for ordinary people to recognise the person as sick. Even the victim himself does not realise that he is sick. He only realises the agony, and believes that this is due to environmental circumstances and feels that if those conditions are changed, he will then be relieved of the agony. But the environment or the circumstances cannot be improved or changed according to his choice. The best way is, to know your inner weaknesses and rectify the shortcomings so that you can meet those exigencies squarely.

Earlier we discussed various types of depression. The Reactive Depression (R.D.) is not hereditary. But the Primary Endogenous Depression (P.E.D.) may sometimes be hereditary. Even educated and intelligent men like Julian Huxley and Winston Churchill suffered from primary endogenous depression.

CHAPTER IV

Yesterday, Today and Tomorrow

By yesterday, today and tomorrow, I mean childhood, youth and old age. I presume that this book will be read mostly by people in the age group of 20 and 45. Generally, youth begins from 25 and ends at 35. And youth is considered the cream of life. But what about life before 20 and after 35? I consider that the period before 20 is the preparation time and after 35 is the consuming time. God has created us to live happily and healthily. As we grow in childhood, we have pleasant and bitter experiences. We learn to be rational about every aspect of life. If we are alert and are able to benefit from pleasant experiences and ignore unpleasant ones, then when we enter the youthful period, we can cash in on those earnings.

I know one woman who is about 40. She lost her husband and both her legs were crushed in a car accident. In her youth, she tried to learn ways of leading a practical and independent life.

When Mrs. Sarkar was in hospital and her legs were given Orthopaedic treatment, she did not get depressed. At that time, both her sons had just completed their studies and not started earning. She was determined to live, walk and work again. She has been in bed for almost a year and now she is always cheerful and thinks positively. She has started walking and even driving her car. Whenever I visited her apartment, I saw her always smiling and bright in bed attended by a maid.

What she did was self-hypnosis. By self-hypnosis you can maintain your youth as well. It is the attitude which matters. Your attitude towards yourself is your greatest resource.

Earlier, in this book, we discussed the type of correct training during adolescence. If your school and parents have taken you through proper channels, you will grow into a perfect youth. Perfect youth implies physical and mental perfection. If you are mentally alert and have good habits, it is probable that you will possess good physical health also, unless you are prone to some hereditary disease.

The Child

The mistake made by most parents and educational institutions is that they want to groom the student to be financially independent. It is advisable and necessary for every human being to work and work efficiently too, so as to make a place in society and survive physically and mentally with self respect. In addition to this grooming, to enable him to live upto commercial and social expectations, he has to have the ability to raise himself to the personality and morality level also.

To enable us to follow this, we are to understand the three *Gunas: Satvas, Rajas* and *Tamas*. These three elements when combined in various proportions comprise the Universe. The *Satvas* contribute to the Conquest of Sloth and neglect; the *Rajas* contribute to the experience of pain and pleasure and the *Tamas* contribute to excessive pleasure. For each guna, different foods and behaviours are indicated. 'Aulukya' propounded a theory similar to that of the atomic theory. Tamas is the property which causes material bodies to remain the same from moment to moment. Tamas, provides material bodies with a static quality of cohesion without which the world would not exist. Tamas renders knowledge static so that it may be stored in the brain.

So, from these we gather that we human beings should inculcate the Trigunas in right proportions which vary from childhood to old age. Some examples may be helpful to clarify the adaptation of the three gunas.

A person following truthfully, the only *Satva Gunas* will probably have to live in an ideal place where he is to speak the truth and do justice and eat and drink only those fruits, vegetables and cereals just sufficient to maintain himself without allowing any untoward reaction on his body and mind. Whereas those following the *Rajas Gunas* will live in a heterogeneous environment and behave like a sovereign and eat the best fruit and food of various types to satiation point and indulge in all sorts of pleasure—seeking devices. And again, a person following *Tamas Gunas* will be greedy and be addicted to so many vices. He will not hesitate to resort to unscrupulous deeds to meet his ends and indulge in odd types of addictions.

To become a personality like the King *Janak*, of our Indian mythological epic Ramayana, who was the King (Raja) as well as Sage (Rishi) and at the same time was an eminent Scholar, we should make special efforts.

Youth

Sigmund Freud (1856-1939) was probably the first psychologist who maintained that child psychology has a bearing on adult psychology and that human nature is the result of interaction among heredity, chance and will. As a physician he staggered the Neo-Victorian world with the theory of personality that saw that all human behaviour is unconsciously motivated by the *Sexual Urge*.

Note that all human beings, means men and women of all ages from childhood to adulthood and into old age. Generally sex is considered a forbidden fruit for all adults. Whether we admit it or not, it is there in all of us all the time and guides us in the shaping of our personality.

Freud divided the mind into three territories:-

(1) The Conscious.

(2) The Pre-conscious (or sub-conscious).

(3) The Unconscious.

At every moment our thoughts are in any of the above territories. There are advantages and disadvantages in all these stages. These stages can be changed or shifted to other stages either by *Yoga, Hypnotism* or by *Drugs*.

Every young man or woman should know that controlling his thoughts and translating them into action is mostly in his own power. But, for this power, the person is to become cultured and develop himself. For this development, he is to know the various stages of mind. In the year 1927, Sigmund Freud established that the three States of mind are:-

(a) Id

(b) Ego

(c) Super Ego

Id, is ruled by the pleasure principle, ego is the cauldron of seething excitement on Id, and super ego is the repository of ideals or morals.

Now, there are various ways of adjustments of the States of your youthful mind, viz.:-

(1) Repression.
(2) Regression.
(3) Aggression.
(4) Fantasy.
(5) Denial.
(6) Protection.
(7) Rationalisation.
(8) Sublimation.

Young man will not find it interesting if we discuss all the factors mentioned. But anybody who is interested may refer to the book, An Introduction to Psychology by - Ralph Norman Haber and Aharon H. Fried.

But a note on the process of self control may be helpful for the young.

We are groomed by our parents, school and environment and are then prepared for our youth. With all these ideas, when we enter youth, we definitely have to know the 'talisman' to outwit evil and emerge from dingy lanes into bright sunshine.

Sigmund Freud believed that all our behaviour is motivated by the tendency to approach pleasure and avoid pain. According to Freud, the pleasure principle governs the physiological responses to the basic drives or instincts such as:-

(a) *Hunger.*

(b) *Thrust.*

(c) *Sex.*

According to him, the function of the nervous system is to reduce excitation to the lowest possible level. We are compelled to obtain the object of the instinct and thereby eliminate the source of conditions of the stimulus, only when the need is satisfied in a manner suited to us, then does the pleasure finally result.

At times, we want more and more excitement and sometimes to the endurance point, and only then are satisfied. This may be in sports, horse racing or even in sex.

We have already discussed that children when groomed, only collect instructions and information. But all these are to be chewed and digested. For that you need maturity. And that maturity comes when you are young.

We have also discussed love and hate, earlier in this book. True love is a compassion for all living things; the yoga ideal. But yoga is not an arid philosophy and does not advocate celibacy, for, only a few of us are equipped to live without a mate. The founders of yoga had wives and children. Except for the few, a normal lovelife is essential for growth as well as mental and spiritual development. Women are the inspiration of men, the 'symbol of the creative power of the universe'.

When you enter the domain of youth, you undergo such biological changes that male and female personalities associate in body and mind respectively. At this crucial period, you must be both cautious and choosy.

As American psychoanalyst, Dr. Carl Jung (1875 - 1961), said that violent love is more often changed into violent hate than to a state of indifference culminating in suicide or killings.

It is often seen that those boys and girls who are in violent love, may consummate their lives ultimately. So, young man, love you must, but you should moderate it. Love one and love all indiscriminately whether it is a human being, male or female, animals, plants or any objects or thoughts.

By love and love only, you can attain perfection, and you can conquer happiness. But is it possible to love everybody or any object, all the time? yes, if at times, when it is not possible to love, then please do not hate either. As soon as you start hating, you are automatically reduced to a second-rate personality. Do you, young man want to submit to that?

It has been found by the Socio-cum-psycho-analysts, that for young persons the age from 18 to 28 is of significance. Most of the miracles or calamities happen specifically during this period.

Another thing you are to keep in mind that generally the brain faculties are at their peak during 28 and 32, and from 32 to 35, it starts drooping slightly and then from 35 onwards the down gradiant is rather steep. Mental and physical decay start at the age of 40 and you should keep abreast with situations and try to give an upthrust to both of them. After 40 you are at the gateway to old age. You should not be ignorant about it. You have already crossed about half of your young life and should then prepare for the next period.

Old Age

After 40, physical and mental decay starts. If you have not lived as suggested earlier in this book, you are liable to be a victim of obesity, blood pressure, gout, insomnia, migraine and may also be a gastitis patient. And, if you wait for a few more years you are to see a doctor for your amoebiasis, or constipation, asthma or even diabetes. If you are not interested in all these names, then continue your yoga exercises even after 40, which you might have started in your early youth. For women the age of 40 and for men 60 are the psychological turning points.

I know a lady who after menopause was mentally so disturbed that she started doubting her husband and beating her children. As she was ignorant about this apprehension and did not prepare for this eventuality, she had to visit a doctor for a long time till she was cured. But what happened was that she lost a few golden years of her life and her husband and others suffered because of her.

Similar hormone change occurs in men also but generally at a slightly advanced age of 60.

Be it men or women, if they have a few hobbies of their choice 10 to 20 years earlier, then they will be pleasantly diverted. The endocrine glands will start functioning to help their bodies and minds to work well in the right direction.

If you have been a bread earner, you are to start planning at the age of 40 for the future. Plan how you propose to sustain yourself and your family, how you will spend the rest of your life and occupation. Do not complain that you have too many liabilities and too few assets. Cut your coat according to your cloth and be happy. If you really have such problems, then there are so many ways out if you can ingeniously plan your budget. After all, so many people have done it before you, then why not you? Nobody will help you except yourself. In many cases, unnecessary timidity makes the trouble worse than it need be.

In childhood, things were otherwise. The children did not know what is want, deprivation or duping. They were fresh like flowers. The real trouble starts during adolescence, and it snowballs in youth. All these problems affect us. And when we enter old age, we cannot go back and change what happened earlier but are left to face the music So, whatever and how much, we can make efforts to sustain ourselves, we should not at all neglect it in our early life. We are to eat balanced food in correct quantity and quality and at correct times, think in a balanced way and take regular physical and mental exercise and rest at proper times.

A few words about love and sex at old age will be discussed in the next chapter.

But before closing, I may say a few words. Before you step into old age, that is before you cross 40, you should remember that the moment youthful animation is gone, you are aged.

Chronologically when you have crossed 40, you are aged. But mentally if you think that you are young, lively, interested and attentive, have a desire to experience and to know, have hobbies and goals, love people and be loved, then you are young again. When you think that you are getting old, try this simple recipe.

Refuse to be a cynic, refuse to criticise, to condemn or be pessimistic. Exult in the wonders of living and the agelessness of time and praise those who are beautiful around you. In short, try this *Self-Hypnosis* and you are *Young* again.

Take the case of Mr. Mathur whom I know. He was a brilliant scholar and a gold medalist. He had a good career in the Administrative Services and was healthy too. After retirement he had no specific hobby to pursue except scores of daily chores. When he lost his position in his career, he was left with his wife and children. Thus, unlike himself his friends differed and broke their ties with him. Eventually, he was so dismayed that he wanted to desert his family, till a granddaughter was born in the family, when his disposition was changed.

How all types of love, can elevate and keep you young again, is discussed in the next chapter.

CHAPTER V

Sex and Work : How Can They Elevate Us

Sex

Sex as well as work, when tackled with modulation can boost your psychology and give you happiness and prosperity.

As mentioned earlier, you cannot ignore sex from birth to death, it is a part of yourself. Anything that belongs to you, must be maintained and utilised profitably and wisely.

When a baby starts sucking *its* thumb, *she* feels the presence of sex and enjoys it. How can you deny it? the awareness of sex comes long before puberty but it is felt, long afterwards, and expressed in ways and means by which others become aware of the change in your metabolism.

But in Indian Society, sex is considered a taboo. Hence a number of people express immaturity in their sexual life, more so than in other fields of human activities and thus they suffer from emotional stress.

Biological urge for food and the desire for security are stronger than the sex instinct. But in the old days, civilised society would have been destroyed, if everybody had been sexually promiscuous. We will have to develop a good educational process for educating the individual, how he can control the instinct within certain restraints.

According to Sigmund Freud, sex is the main spring of human personality. To meet the need for food and shelter is not so difficult as to curb the sexual urge wisely. Sex is a biological instinct, and to modulate the sexual urge is difficult, more because many commercial enterprises are deliberately arousing people's sexual desires to meet their personal ends. Growing personalities specially, young boys and girls, should keep in mind that:-

"It is easier to stay out of trouble than to get out of it if you are in."

Elders generally disregard sex and make a distinction between it and the desire for food and shelter in such a manner that the young and adolescents are apprehensive when ordered to abstain from this activity. Then their sex curiosity is heightened and things take an ugly shape.

Sex is a tough problem. You cannot possibly put a cork in the bottle of a pressure vessel. If you do, you run the risk of the cork blowing off or the bottle bursting. Either the pressure may be reduced or diverted to avoid the catastrophe. If it is not taken care of, well in time, then your excited sexual desires will imbibe emotional stresses and probably you will end in some legal trouble; or your children may get into wrong emotional patterns and habits.

We should, therefore, introduce courses of studies in the schools for educating the students about the human physiology and the basic do's and dont's of sexual activities. The co-education in schools and colleges should also be encouraged which will eliminate the unethical sexual urge promoting mental tension and a gloomy future.

With basic guidance and sex education, when you are young, you know what sex is and how it should be handled. Though, love and sex pervades all your life from birth to death, yet at the same time you should know that sex and love are two different entities, connected by a thin thread. You may pull the thread but not break it.

Again love and hate are two sides of the same coin. Follow one of the two maxims: "Love and do not hate or don't hate but only love". Love starts from inside your mother's womb and it continues till you die. The first explicit love starts from your mother's care and caressings. When you grow older, you start loving shapes and colours, the sun, moon, the breeze, the twittering of birds, the bristle of the leaves on the trees, the murmuring of the fallen leaves, the whistling of the wind through the branches of the threes, the roaring of the sea, and so on.

When you are a little older, you get thrilled when little children run to you with open hands. You are filled with love and joy. The stimulus of love is released from your emotion.

The endocrine glands get tuned, hormones flow, the facial muscles draw up, your heart beats faster and the aura of youthfulness invades your body. You, not only feel younger, but due to hormone flow, your ageing process is decelerated.

When you grow still older, and are married, you get similar elations from your spouse and your children or even from your domestic pets. You are to create an attitude for it. This way you forget over-indulgence in the matter of sexual activities and love pervades you more than the sexual urge.

Talking of sexual activities, if you can adjust rhythm with your spouse, you will have a mature love and will have eternal satisfaction. (More details are outside the scope of this book.)

People think that sexual advancement is a sort of sophistication. But in reality, it is a sexual immaturity which leads to Emotionally Induced Illness (E.I.I.) culminating in mental and physical diseases.

In early youth, people cannot discriminate between the desire to eat and the sexual urge. You have the curiosity to know more of sex. To the young, sex is as new as some new food or fruit. It is for the elders to give proper knowledge and guidance to the young. This is not always possible for the parents for obvious reasons. If the schools and other educational institutions do not give proper education to them in this respect, it is very natural that they will try to obtain commercial books and literature to get salacious and dubious information and therefore be misled.

The sex urge is a natural instinct. It is not to be discouraged or hated, but profitably it can be controlled and channelised. This is possible if the young person is helped to become proficient in sports, or be skilled in handicrafts or engaged in any community enterprise. This way the results of such pursuits will serve to enable the young person to forget much of the time that he is a sexual animal. It will also develop general and mental maturity, helping to sublimate the sex urge to a secondary level. This can best be done by the family as well as by the School and the Community Centres.

In Hindu philosophy, we find that we should marry for progeny only. But the very thought of or association with your spouse stimulates your *Pituitary Gland* to activate the endocrine glands. Hormones flow as a result, irrigating the whole body, thus imparting physical and mental health. Sexual relationship in marriage should be a cooperative enterprise. It is unique and ideal if your actions are pleasant to both partners and enjoyed by both. This way both members respond and acquire a better understanding. They ultimately so intermingle with each other that they are indistinguishable and become truly one through the years. This way there is every chance of both members being healthy, physically and mentally.

Work

It is said that "Work is Worship". That is you may reach God if you work. At least you may acquire godly qualities. It is also said that "an idle mind is the devils' workshop." Both maxims are correct, but how do you justify these?

It was discussed earlier in this chapter that society will disgrace you for over-indulgence in sexual activities, and you will become a victim of Emotionally Induced Illness (E.I.I.).

Suppose you are kept in a room comfortably, with food and other amenities, but are debarred from work or to speak to anybody, then very soon you will get bored and you will feel as if you are pushed into a great void. You may get mentally sick to such a degree, that you may develop psycho-somatic diseases. And after sometime, when the 'being sick' stage is over, you may get real sickness, and you may be a diseased man.

Work is essential not only to earn your bread but to prevent boredom. Most of the idle-rich suffer immense boredom as a price for their freedom from drudgery. It is also seen that more intelligent, rich men work nearly as hard as if they were poor. And also most of the intelligent, rich women keep themselves busy, with innumerable trifles. Work, therefore, is indispensable, first and foremost, as a preventive measure for boredom.

For most of paid work and for some unpaid work also, the ambition is for success; and most of those are measured by the income earned. A good income brings in better comforts, and possibly better pleasure. Reputation is another aspect for which men are inclined to work. If the work is interesting, a man will tend to devote more energy and time which will give him great satisfaction, and he will try to acquire more skills and try to achieve perfection. But, there is a limit to it. There are also innumerable ways to create interest in work, which is limitless.

There are three types of work, viz., constructive, destructive and neutral. An architect, a writer, a painter, a singer or a cook, all work constructively. But the man who is engaged in demolishing buildings or destroying debris or take the case of the butcher — they all work towards a destructive end. Both these groups of men or women earn their wages as well as their satisfaction. They have their pleasure and thereby have emotional statis also.

In this respect, the women who are only housewives are much less fortunate than men or those women who also work outside the home. In short, even men or women whose work is dull and is of a neutral nature, yet are happier than those who have no work at all.

Generally, it is seen that eminent artists and great men of science create pieces of work which delight them as well as give them satisfaction and ultimately make them happy. Sometimes, it is also seen that there are people who produce pieces of work of immense beauty or utility out of agony. Had it not been due to this agony, it would not have been possible for them to produce such a piece of perfection. Lenin created order out of chaos, Michelangelo was a profoundly unhappy man. Had he not been in agony, he probably could not have created such great art that will be remembered for ages.

Often, it is seen that rich corporations directed by philistines insist upon producing nonsense with the help of intellectual giants to meet their ends. Hence, it is always advisable that whenever it is possible to do work to his own satisfaction without absolutely starving, he should, for his own happiness, quit such highly remunerative jobs, and switch to work of his own choice. This enables him, to achieve satisfaction and happiness so as to enjoy Emotional Statis.

Another thing you should note, that "All work and no play makes a dull boy", is a fitting maxim. Whether it is money, reputation or satisfaction that you are getting out of your work, you must reserve some time and energy for physical exercise and recreation, both of which are necessary for a perfect personality.

Achieving job satisfaction is not due to the nature or the quantum of work, but is entirely dependent on the attitude of the worker. We have seen earlier, that the job may be of any nature, but it is the person performing the task who is more important. You may not be proud, but you should have enough pride to see the project through and complete it satisfactorily.

The brain is the centre of thought. Sorrow, joy, vanity and desire for power and wealth, are all fed on egoism. The more we feed the ego, the farther we get away from the real self. Many of our actions are due to the underlying forces which are born in the unconscious mind. It is this *Avidya* which must be dissipated by concentration, meditation and at the end by contemplation. In this way, we can control our minds, instead of letting our minds control us. Having achieved this, we can concentrate on selfless work, which will give us satisfaction, pleasure and happiness. This, ultimately can give us 'emotional statis' and save us from Emotionally Induced Illness (E.I.I.).

Some people regard their life as a whole and to others life is a series of detached incidents disjointed and not focussed on one goal. The former group of people mostly achieve happiness and derive contentment and self respect.

To view life as a whole, is an essential part of wisdom and true morality. This attitude may be imbibed through programmed and channelised education. Determination and single mindedness are indispensable conditions of a happy life. These are achieved only through sincere work.

CHAPTER VI

Old Age is A Golden Age

Old people generally look back nostalgically on those golden days left behind. You cannot possibly reverse the clock, but you can give those added hours and days of life, a new meaning.

Old age is a golden age — yes, if you can maintain it. There are outside agents which will try to pull you down, but if you are careful, you can hold it up to a considerable extent.

About 100 years ago, most people lived upto the age of 60 to 65, with the exception of a few. But with the turn of the century, the average life expectancy will go up to 70 to 80.

With the progress of science and advancement of literacy, people have managed to lead a healthy life and have greater longevity. But our question is not only to live a healthier, but to lead a happier life too.

In old age, our negative emotions tend to be on the higher side, due to financial insecurity, health hazards and worry about the future. With the advent of old age, we also suffer from apprehension, disappointment and discouragement which boost our negative emotions. These negative emotions or stresses, as we call them, excite the pituitary gland to produce *Somato-Trophic Hormones* (S.T.H.). These hormones have adverse effects on us. Thus, the degenerative diseases so produced are on the higher side due to increased emotional stresses, of modern times. The cause of these degenerative diseases are two fold, it may either be emotionally induced or due to aging of the organs and tissues.

As far as my studies go, about 70 percent of these degenerative diseases are emotionally - induced. Hence, if we take care of our psychology before entering old age, (say when we have not reached 50), then the whole picture will emerge differently.

For example, menopause generally occurs when women are in their forties. In some, groups of people the range is from 38 to 55, while for others, it may be in the age group from 45 to 50. Menopause is due to the normal ending of uterine bleeding owing to the natural aging of the ovaries, which causes the *Estrogenic Female Hormones* to flow. Due to the menopause, most women have minor physical and psychological disturbances during this time: generally the body temperature suddenly rises and then returns to normal. Other symptoms are irritability, insomnia, dizziness and depression. The skin becomes inelastic and wrinkles may start developing over the body and pubic hair also recedes. This is the time when a woman should raise her spirits and not allow herself to be depressed or suffer from an inferiority complex.

During this period, she should divert herself from her usual routine and get involved in other habits and hobbies to keep her body and mind fully engaged so that she can always remain cheerful.

It is a fact that women outlive men, but very few enjoy their longevity. Failure of the glands of internal secretion has been linked to old age. Failure of one endocrine gland contributes to the failure of another. This the mechanism by which old age advances. Men, whose endocrine glands function normally, experience no trouble in their *Prostate Gland*. They stay young, sexually and otherwise also. Their skin remains looking young.

Aging, premature or on schedule is a matter of self-maintenance. When health rules are violated by bad habits, such as excessive smoking or sex, alcoholism or malnutrition, the chain of health breaks down. When physical resistance retreats, bacteria and infections creep in. Or otherwise, when someone has emotional problems while trying to reach his goal, this deep-seated urge may be converted into serious organic or functional diseases. He has obviously not learnt how to cope with his own tensions.

Physical aging begins when the elasticity of muscles and ligaments start failing, when the skin shows sags and folds, when sexual desire declines, when memory begins to fail and ability to learn slows down, when the mechanisms of sight and hearing do not cooperate, when insomnia begins, when the joints and muscles start paining. Then you know that you are getting old. It is possible to delay this trail of agony.

Take the case of the skin first. Be it for men or women, regular physical exercises, local or general, can retain the skin glow considerably, if you supplement these with a proper balanced diet, containing enough minerals, vitamins and pure water. Massage, with oil, ointment or free hand may be used regularly, specially with the advent of old age. Along with it, free hand exercise and walking or jogging is an added advantage.

I used the word regularly. This means that vigorous exercise once in a while will do more harm than help. As the athletes have to have year-round training and exercise, to keep young and energetic, you should follow a schedule of exercise all the year round, and all the time, you should convince yourself that you are young and have a long way to go.

Sexual desire declines with old age and so you abstain more from the sexual act. The whole system deteriorates and runs down. You do not see beauty in beautiful things. You do not appreciate a piece of art. If you are a man, you probably develop asthma or enlarged prostate glands. Then, you are sure to have entered old age. If you are not debarred from the sexual act, because of some other physical illnesses, or if you have not lost your spouse, then you should make it a point to have elation as previously, but with modulated frequency and intensity - as a sustenance dose only. If you are a woman, then you can behave similarly, but in somewhat different ways; because the sex urge of men and women are not exactly similar. Even if you have advanced into old age, you can supplement similar emotions, by talking, behaving and other activities. Men or women can continue to have emotional statis by working together, playing together or exchanging thoughts or going out to places together.

The urge to learn and the memory may decline. But both of them may be delayed considerably by regular exercise of the mind.

Take the case of Dr. *Nirad C. Choudhury*, the world-renowned author. Now in Britain (since 1970), this renowned enfant terrible of Indian writers in English, was born in East Bengal and after completing his studies from Calcutta University, was employed in the Military Accounts Department at Calcutta in 1920. He had aspirations and he worked all the time to achieve an honourable position in society. So, he left Government Service after a few years, to become a free-lance journalist during World War II.

Before leaving for London, when I visited his place, I saw a special sparkle in his eyes. One day, while talking to me in his study, where books were stacked from floor to the ceiling, he suddenly rushed out into the ante-room. To keep me company, his wife came in and resumed our conversation. When I asked her where and why he rushed out, she smiled and replied that he was always in a trance, and allowed me to look into the room where he was seen deeply engrossed in writing, with open books all round him. This has ultimately rewarded him. In his 93rd year of life, he was awarded the Honorary Doctor of Letters by Oxford University on March 3, 1989. He was the fifth Indian to have an honorary D. Litt. from Oxford University. I am familiar with his simple living and food habits, even during his sojourn in London. His organised life and cultivation of knowledge have enabled him to live a healthy and a happy existence. This is one of the many such examples.

With the advancement of age, when the mechanism of sight and hearing decline, you have nothing to do except procuring mechanical aids to supplement those lost assets. But, if you are cautious at an early stage, you can effectively arrest or delay the process of the aging of these mechanisms. There are very appropriate processes and exercises for rejuvenating both the organs in yoga. Follow these rules and practice these exercises, well in time, and see the result. There are several do's and don'ts that if followed, will keep you young and keep you free of troublesome ailments.

For the joints and muscles, the exercises recommended earlier for owning a beautiful skin and a youthful gait are applicable here too.

Emotions are generally the product of the mind, and hence the mind can be trained to discard the negative emotions, and save yourself from the grip of old age. Walk away from the source of trouble physically and mentally and you are safe.

Analysing the cause of our depression, we see that of all the humiliating and depressing factors, financial insecurity is the one which is most prominent. An earning member is almost at his peak at the age of 50. He should plan his future budget in such a way that he can "cut his coat according to the cloth available to him." The planning should be down to earth. He should stop progeny after 35 and after each child birth, a small compulsory saving should follow, so that he is not to worry when the child is 15 or 20 years of age. After 40, the travelling expenses and all other extravagant expenses should be rationed. New purchases and gifts should be reduced. If you want fewer worries in old age, then start these right now, before you are 50.

Job security and the establishment in society, are other factors he worries about. Older persons, surely have less dexterity and promptness which amounts to less productivity; but on the other hand, due to their experience and maturity, they are more helpful as regards the quality of the job and administration. You cannot just throw away the old. They are assets to the family, to industry and to the nation. This is quite correct, but you are to live upto it and prove it. However, you are not debarred from thinking and feeling that you are more mature and useful than the younger generation, in many ways. This will also give you emotional statis.

Regarding the behaviour and presentation, generally the old seem to be more abrupt and assertive in their talk and appearance; thereby they are rejected by others. Maybe, he was as bitter or acerbic in his twenties or thirties. But probably at that age, his behaviour and faults were camouflaged or compensated by his walk, gestures, appearance or fluency of speech. When the external qualities diminish, you should make an attempt to improve upon your other qualities to compensate those lost, in old age.

By dint of love and hate experiences, during your earlier life, you have learnt, whether and how much you gain or lose by love or hate. Now, during old age, you have the chance to cash in on those experiences.

Thirty-five is the age when our brain faculties start deteriorating. We gradually start sinking and by the time, we reach the age of 45 or 50, we generally develop a feeling that the earth has disappeared from under our feet. This is the time when we should brush up our faculties and give an upthrust to our activities, so as not to allow defeat to creep in. We should revise and revamp our mental attitudes.

If you have not already included a few hobbies in your schedule of work at the age of 35, then you must do it from the age of 40 definitely. Consider the age of 35 to 45 as the transition period, when you must brush up all your activities and re-arrange them to meet the next phase of life.

Some people complain that the age of 35 to 45 is the prime time to work, then how do they waste time and energy on trifling hobbies and recreations? But for developing hobbies, you do not have to have extra time and energy. Primarily, hobbies and recreation may be merged to a large extent in the work itself. By doing this, the work itself will be so much more interesting. If you think that you can plan some hobby and recreation outside the work, well and good. Both things are indispensable for a healthy body and mind. There can be several safe and innocent recreations which need less time and money. The recreations and hobbies may be so chosen that they build up a healthy body and mind. Many of these can be creative and entertaining, such as music, painting, reading, writing and gardening. Whereas, smoking, drinking, drug addiction, and polygamy are destructive pasttimes which will ultimately ruin you.

If you want to remain young and agile, you should be associated with the younger generation more than the old. Try it out for a few months and you will observe that it gives you a ballistic swing. Younger groups of people are more active and optimistic and hence an association with them will give you a fillip to life. Move with younger people, laugh with them and you will forget your blues. The blues may be there, but they will not remind you constantly of their existence. *You are as Old as you Think you are.*

Mental and physical aging slow down when people are associated with small children, domestic pets and birds and are fond of flowers and gardening. After some research, it was found that if you associate, with and are fond of people of the opposite sex and indulge in tender things, the secretion of the glands (endocrine ductless glands) are regulated and balanced. The organs function in an orderly manner and you feel younger and happier.

Many quacks claim that few tablets and potions will give you youth and happiness. These are all unnatural ways. They do more harm than good. Sometimes, they over stimulate your glands and send you nowhere and then you don't have the way to return.

To prolong youth and happiness, you have no short cut or quick methods. You have to work on it in a determined and methodical way, which will be dealt with in the last two chapters.

Love and compassion for others and the ability to compromise, will help you to acquire positive healthy emotions, thereby enabling you to have emotional statis. If you follow this doctrine, it will do you and others good. Those who come into contact with you, will feel happy and elated.

In old age, since you are not compelled to work vigorously to earn your living, you will have enough spare time. But this is not a boon, but a curse. Idle time is the Devil's Workshop. You will think wrongly, do wrong deeds and ultimately suffer for all these. So why not spend your time in something creative, or amusing and turn your old age to a golden age?

CHAPTER VII

The Cause, Prevention and Remedy

You cannot separate body and mind. Soma, the body and psyche, the mind, are two inter-dependent and inseparable entities.

From early childhood, we should take care of the body by maintaining proper health rules and a balanced diet, consumed at regular intervals.

Some parents think that vigorous exercise, followed by a sumptuous meal, rich in calories and proteins will help in building a bony baby, who will grow into a solid personality.

By hard physical exercise the child may develop firm muscles and by consuming rich and sumptuous meals, the child may develop a pulpy body and most likely will be prone to frequent illness. What the child needs is yoga, and not the stereotyped hard mundane exercises. Of course, exercise in some form should be as much a part of the daily routine, as eating. It is recommended that instead of the routine physical exercises, he should go in for outdoor games of any sort for body warming. Physical exercise of this sort will bring about psychological maturity and social awareness. With the advent of age, he should change the type of exercises too. For example, swimming, jogging or walking at an advanced age, are suitable exercises. Of course, there is a slight variation in the pattern of games played and exercises done for male and female members for a number of reasons. However, there are such a wide

variety of yoga exercises, that they can be selected separately for all ages and sexes. These exercises are not violent ones and are designed to use the muscles and activate the internal organs and tissues to the graded amount only, which can be modulated for each individual. Yoga exercises are beneficial for the body as well as the mind. By yoga, I mean not the Hatha Yoga, but the Raj Yoga also.

For performing yoga, it is recommended that it should be started with a clean body, clean mind, and with neat clothes on. Body hygiene is of absolute necessity for this process.

But amazingly, it is seen that inspite of proper exercises and balanced food, people do fall a victim to physical illnesses. This may sometimes be due to environmental and ecological reasons, which possibly, you cannot control.

For example, the food you eat may contain toxins due to the fertilisers used in growing them or due to the deficient processing methods before all these reach your doorstep. You can avoid a few ill effects by avoiding some of the foods thus processed and by supplementing those by some other food or by processing your food by improved methods.

The environment affects the quality of the food eaten by us. Even if it is processed properly, the question is, whether it is consumed at proper times or intervals or in proper quantities. Is the food that is eaten, a balanced diet? Has the 'Coat been cut according to your size'? Otherwise, you will have the feeling of "having your feet in another man's shoes".

If you are interested to know all about your diet, in detail, you may refer it to the following organisation who will provide you with all the requisite information.

Technical Adviser,
Ministry of Agriculture,
Department of Food,
Food and Nutrition Board,
Northern Region,
Government of India,
New Delhi.

Now, you know, what food and how much in quantity, you are to take at what age and sex, and according to your profession, in order to be physically healthy. But it is not so simple.

It is also important as to what your physical and mental condition is before and after you eat your food. A few simple rules laid down by the "Iron Man of Bengal", Nirod Sarkar are given below:-

1. You may take a thin soup or pure water, half an hour before consuming your square meals. But while taking food, you may have a few sips also, if you cannot avoid it.

Then half an hour after your meals, you should drink a full glass of water, for correct digestion and assimilation of the food consumed.

2. Before and while eating your food, you should be free from mental tension, agony or anger. You may delay your meals, if you are perturbed due to these reasons.

3. You should masticate your food properly, before you gulp, because your saliva helps you to convert the starchy food into sugar by the enzymes in the mouth.

4. It is a bad practice to discuss grave problems while taking your food. You may just appreciate and enjoy the food.

5. However bad the food, you should never complain about it, either you can eat it or leave it, but not hate it.

6. Fill your stomach to 3/4th full only, because otherwise there will be no space left for churning it for digestion.

7. After the food, you should take at least 20 minutes rest or have a light walk and any hard labour may be done only after 30 to 40 minutes after your meals.

8 Meals at night should be lighter and at the scheduled timings only and not after 22 hours in any case.

9. Avoid cold milk and hot, sour dishes (*Khattas* and Chutneys). Never drink milk after eating fish, meat or eggs.

10. At night, after food, you should rest for about an hour before retiring to bed. Better, if you can do Bajrasan and then Sabasan before going to sleep.

11. At night, curd and *ghee* (fat) should be avoided.

12. Plan to take mostly alkaline food. Excessive acid in food gives rise to diseases like, asthma, gout or cancer. Lemon, when consumed, works like an alkali inside our body.

13. Fasting is recommended at least once or twice a month. Lemon water with a pinch of salt in it, may be taken during fasting and the fast may be broken in the afternoon or night by consuming light food like citrus fruit juices, vegetable soup or lemon water.

Swami Shivananda Swaraswati, a yogic exponent, maintains that in a hot country like ours, children upto the age of 5 should not take fish, prepared sweets (*mithai*); and upto the age of 10, food such as ghee, butter, meat and eggs are detrimental for a growing child. By not abiding by this rule, children from the age of 10 or 15 suffer from liver trouble. Food may be supplemented with ample milk, curd, greens and other vegetables and various types of fruit. If this routine is maintained upto the age of 20 to 25, then the body will be sturdy enough to withstand various undulations.

If all these methods listed are followed properly from childhood, you will emerge into a healthy and mature young man or woman.

Maturity and Anger

Along with a strong and flawlessly healthy body, we need a strong and healthy mind too. Lack of maturity will lead to bouts of depression. Depression will follow from mental tension and anxiety and all these may be due to the lack of maturity. It is not necessary that maturity will come with age, but it is expected to. But do not wait for it. Develop maturity from childhood.

A person may be well educated, earning well or may be an expert in one trade or the other, but it is still possible that he may be lacking in maturity.

Anger is one of the serious ailments due to anxiety and depression. An angry man and a man who is drugged or drunk are almost in the same group. He can commit any type of crime which is unethical or irreligious, culminating in irrevocable deeds which may be harmful for society or even to himself. Hence, to control anger is our primary problem.

Soon after depression sets in, distrust and hatred develop. When you cannot reconcile yourself to life, anger emerges, develops and shows its colours.

If you are frustrated or defeated in any circumstances, try to analyse the issue on a piece of paper in columns as cause, effect and remedy. Then try to sleep over it for sometimes. Then again revise it and follow the rules noted below:

Three golden rules are:-

(1) Natural elusion or avoidance of cause.

(2) Change of environment.

(3) Counselling or self-analysis.

If you find the first one is difficult then move on to the next. Leave the site of your frustration. Temporary involvement in other activities like solving crossword puzzles or having some serious studies or going out for a stroll may help you. Follow anyone that suits you. This will relieve you of a lot of problems and the tension is, to a great extent, minimised. The third method is self-analysis or counselling. This is done by analysing the cause and effect issues. Have a debate with your conscience. You will definitely find a solution to it.

If this Self-analysis does not work and the patient becomes a victim of depression repeatediy, then he is to see a physician and later, if necessary, see a psychiatrist.

The Depression

If the depression is not congenital or due to some organic defeats or deformities; these are curable, if cared for at an early stage. Otherwise, these may develop into acute mental diseases. The physician will be able, after analysis, to diagnose as to whether it is hereditary or functional.

The Reactive Depression (R.D.) discussed in the earlier chapters, are not hereditary. But the Primary Endogenous Depression (P.E.D.) are found to be hereditary in many cases. Educated and intelligent people like Julian Huxley and Winston Churchill also suffered from Primary Endogenous Depression (P.E.D.).

Mild melancholy due to R.D. should not be neglected. If the patient tries *Self-Analysis*, at an early stage, then with a minimum effort he may come round. Otherwise, if he is left in his depressed state for a long time, this may take a form of Secondary Endogenous Depression (S.E.D.). If the patient drifts from R.D. to S.E.D., then he becomes less reactive to counselling.

It is also seen that in Reactive Depression (R.D.), the number of women patients in our society are almost double the number of men patients. But for the Endogenous Depression (E.D.) patients, both men and women have a fairly equal share.

They are from the cream of our society—educated, sophisticated and affluent.

I had come across an elderly lady who was declared an almost incurable heart patient. When hospitalised, I visited her and found her so depressed that she gave up all hopes of survival.

Mrs. R. Chakravorty, a widow, and a school teacher, waved me a last farewell when I first went to see her in hospital. Seeing the state of her depression, I generated confidence and convinced the patient that she was curable. In a few days, I found that my counselling had shown results. After she was released from the hospital sometimes later, I used to visit her almost everyday at least once. Gradually she reduced her sleeping drugs and other medicines and finally slept without any sedative. After sometime, she came all the way walking to my residence to thank me for saving her life. As a matter of fact, only the counselling worked and activated in releasing the requisite hormones to revive her health again. She lived for another 15 years.

Live with the Enemy

According to the Indian tradition there are six *Reepus* or *Enemies* in our psyche. They are Kaam, Krodh, Loove, Moho, Mada, Matsarya. The English equivalents are lust, anger, avarice, delusion, pride and envy. They are called the enemies or demons. But you cannot eliminate them altogether, nor can you live a common man's life if you try to shed them totally. A few men had left or controlled some of these to a considerable extent, but not all. If Swami Vivekananda could not eliminate them, nor was Mahatma Gandhi perfect in this respect, why waste time and energy in fighting them? As a matter of fact, if you want to live a successful life and be a happy man, you should try to have a mixture of all the six *Reepus* in graded and controlled amounts.

Learn a lesson from the animals too. The animals have a particular mating age or a certain time of the season, whereas for human beings the year round, at any time of day is mating time. The animals do not harm or attack others unless they are disturbed at meal times or milking time. They do not kill, until they are physically hungry. Whereas men are jealous in many ways and are aggressive on many occasions at the slightest provocation or even without any reasonable cause.

Walt Whitman Wrote

"I think, I could turn and live with animals,

They are placid and self-contained,

They do not sweat and whine about their condition,

They do not lie awake in the dark and weep for their sins,

Not one is dissatisfied, not one is demented . . . .

. . . . with the mania of owning things.

Not one is respectable or unhappy over the whole earth . . . .

. . . ."

We have many valuable things to learn from:

(a) The animals and birds.

(b) The Child.

(c) Nature.

Look, they are so simple and so pure.

In spite of all these sermons and cautions, if you have problems and these are unsolved, and you are unhappy and depressed, then you should find a cure for your melancholy and unhappiness.

All men are a mixture of two elements. He is either an introvert or an extrovert or a mixture of both in variable degrees under different circumstances.

If you have got interests in external affairs, it will give you pain in learning about the calamities that are happening in the world. But these pains do not destroy the essential qualities of your life. Whereas, the internal interests, or those interests in oneself, leads to no activity of a progressive kind and you will be alleviated of ennui or boredom.

In an extreme case, you may be a monk, but you too will not become happy unless your monastery and preachings have made you forget your own soul. External discipline is the only path to happiness for those unfortunates whose self-absorption is too profound to be cured in any other way. The various types being:-

(a) The Sinner

(b) The Narcissist

(c) The Megalomaniac.

A sinner is a person who is absorbed in consciousness of sin, perpetually incurring his own disapproval. He learnt at his mothers' knee that swearing, drinking and sex are all sins; his sense of sin may be buried deep into his unconsciousness and emerges only at times when he is in seclusion or asleep.

Narcissism consists of the habits of admiring oneself and wishing to be admired. Upto a point, it is normal, but the excess of it becomes an evil. A person whose sole concern is that the world should admire him, is not likely to achieve his object. Vanity, when it passes beyond a point, kills pleasure in every activity for its own sake and thus leads to listlessness and boredom.

The megalomaniac wishes to be powerful and seeks to be feared rather than loved. These men are foolish, or unhappy or both. Think of Alexander the Great, Napoleon or even Adolf Hitler. If you look into or analyse their private lives, were they happy?

Going back to the theory of Sigmund Freud, the great Austrian physician, we find that the typical unhappy man is one who has been deprived in youth, of some normal satisfaction. However, there is a development in the adults in the present society, that every man feels thwarted and that he seeks no form of satisfaction and ultimately becomes a devotee of pleasure. That is, he seeks to make life bearable by becoming less active. As, I have mentioned earlier, these frustrated people who indulge in drinking, drugs or in unethical sex relations, are ultimately bored, frustrated, depressed and unhappy.

The Cure

We have discussed at length why and how depression and ultimately, unhappiness win us over. Some methods were also discussed for prevention of these. But if at all, you feel depressed, let us know the ways out.

A few methods to cure depression are listed below:-

1. Circumstantial Methods.
2. Self-Analysis, Meditation and Yoga.
3. Substitution Therapy.
4. Group Therapy.
5. Counselling and Psychoanalysis.
6. Colour, Shape, Music and Gem Therapy.
7. Physical Methods:-
   (a) Drug Therapy.
   (b) Vitamin Therapy.
   (c) E.C.T. Therapy.

If the disease has attacked you, you must counter charge it with skill so as to eliminate the evil in you. The first three methods may be tried by a patient who is trained to tackle the problem, but for the remaining four, further skills are required to treat the patient.

(1) Circumstantial Methods

If you are angry or depressed, try to change your geographical position and your physical or mental environment which will reduce the intensity of your agony. Try to avoid the cause of the trouble, then you are cured.

(2) Self Analysis

The next is self-analysis. You must talk to yourself, your conscience, and discover who was wrong and why, and find a solution to it. If that helps, you may sit down with paper and pencil. All these become easier if you can meditate in oblivion and isolation. Start with *dharana* (concentration) which will lead you to *dhyana* (meditation). By this, you will easily reveal your inner self and find a solution.

(3) Substitution Therapy

The substitution therapy is applicable to a number of cases for different age groups and for typical cases also.

This is seen in small children, if a baby weeps over a broken doll, counselling does not help her. If that doll is substituted by another better doll or teddy bear or a toy aeroplane, she will "forget the agony" of the first doll she was weeping for. In adults, similar cases are dealt with from different angles. Mother forgets some tragedy in the family, when a new baby is born. Sometimes, it is seen that a lady become grim when friends leave her temporarily. However, her pleasure is renewed if some other friend drops in at her home or telephones her. She has to fall back on some other thing, a substitute, for forgetting the agony of the first. It is not always possible for the patient to search for a substitute. Hence in more cases than not, outside help is required to assist her, preferably a psychiatrist's help.

(4) Group Therapy

Some two million years ago, mankind lived in small groups. Gradually, they divided into smaller clusters and lived in small village communities. With the advent of civilisation, people further divided. In India, even about 100 years ago, people lived in joint families. Economically and psychologically they led much happier lives than us who now prefer small families.

In group living, there is a great deal of give and take. Small ripples in the family are smoothened out by higher waves. If a person suffers from depression in a joint family, there are others who can pacify or share his agony and relieve the patient from depression. In the present society, man prefers to live as an isolated unit in a vast community. But when it comes to living with small groups of people who are known to him and are his equal, he feels comfortable. The togetherness and the sense of belonging helps them to survive hardship and overcome depression to a considerable extent.

In South Africa, it was experimented in a hospital, that unpromising patients were put in small groups and were given all sorts of facilities of daily living, as well as various activities, under guidance of trained nurses. These groups were given marks and were promoted to higher groups with better amenities according to their behaviour. This group therapy proved effective and finally, every week cured patients were discharged from the hospital in groups.

(5) Psychotherapy

Before the beginning of the present century, innumerable medicines came to the doctors' rescue. Chemical and microscopic analysis also enabled the doctors to ascertain the disease and find a remedy for physical diseases. But, the patients who had depression or mania or schizophrenia, when their brain cells were examined under the microscope, showed no change or any symptom. No pathological explanation could be arrived at.

At this stage, medical science almost came to a halt for investigating the cause and to find a remedy for patients who suffered from depression, mania or schizophrenia. In the early half of this century, the Austrian physician, Sigmund Freud devised a new method of interpretation and treatment, called *Psychoanalysis*. The patient had to visit the therapist in his clinic and lay relaxed comfortably in a couch, in a dimly lighted room and by free association and counselling with the therapist, the psychological problems of the patient were slowly revealed. The patient himself would in the end discover, where in infancy or in early life, his psychic development had gone wrong. The whole mental structure would be re-built from there in a more stable and mature way.

To be treated under the guidance of a psychiatrist, is not only a time-consuming affair, but is also very costly. I myself took about eleven months to cure a patient in Delhi. The case history is given in Chapter II.

(6) Colour, Shape, Music and Gem Therapy

It has been established by the Colour engineers by studying the use of colours in industry, educational institutions, offices, residential buildings, stores, hotels and hospitals, that colour consists of electromagnetic waves. These have got physiological and psychological reactions on us.

Historically speaking, we find that the first coloured advertisement appeared in 1893. Thereafter, more multi-coloured advertisements were fashionable in the period from 1910 to 1930.

To illustrate how colour affects the human mind, it may be quoted that in those days when people become colour-conscious, the *Blackfriars* Bridge in London was repainted from black to green.

The result was that suicidal deaths of those jumping from the bridge decreased by 33 percent. Professional colour engineer, Howard Ketchun showed that colour has more than aesthetic value. It has an emotional impact as well on us. This can enhance the utility as well as the appeal of the many products and can pay realistic dividends in great employee safety and general well being. It had also been established that colour can translate the emotion into odour, sound and shape. Colour technologists graded them for perception of odour in the descending order as given below:-

Rose, lilac, pine, lily, violet, coffee, etc. Sir Isac Newton experimented with colour and found the association of colour with musical notes (C,D,E,F,G,A,B) such as given below:-

Red with the Scale (C),

Orange (D),

Yellow (E),

Green (F),

Blue (G),

Indigo (A) and

Violet (B)

The most amazing aspect of his experiment was, in study of 148 students, 60 percent of them experienced some kind of colour and when musical notes were heard by them, 39 percent of them were able to see colour.

Colour gives a feeling of shape also as sketched below:-

R	= Red	= Square, solid, hot,dry.
O	= Orange	= Rectangular (upright), warm, incandescent.

= Yellow = Sharp (angular), crisp.

= Green = Sharp cornered, pervading.

= Blue = Circle, sphere - cold, wet, receding.

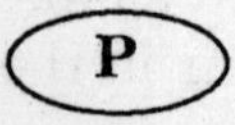

= Purple = Soft, flowering, never clearly seen.

Some language and emotion is also revealed from a particular colour. A few are listed below:-

Red = Passionate—Exciting.

Blue = Indispensable—Subduing.

Green = Jealousy—Tranquillity.

Yellow = Scoundrel— Cheerful.

Some moods are depicted according to the Colours as shown below

R

Exciting

Y

Cheerful

G

Tranquil

B

Subduing

Let us digress a little, to understand the approach to the psyche and to have control over it from an unusual angle.

The world we see, as well as the world we cannot see, are all part of the cosmic force. It is made up of electromagnetic waves of a much higher order and power than we are able to see with our naked eyes. When the sun's rays are split up, we see basically seven primary colours, viz., violet, indigo, blue, green, yellow, orange and red (*Vibgyor*), which is only a visible part of the full cosmic spectrum. Occulists point out, that the mystic number seven comes up everywhere; in colour, in notes (musical), in number of days in a week and so on. In ancient times, the Egyptian population was not taught the complete doctrine of light, but they were taught only the basic primary colours - red, yellow and blue, which correspond to the body, soul (mind) and spirit of human beings. This theory has not yet been discarded. As we have seen earlier that each colour has got a different effect on us, it may be that a particular colour attracts one and the same colour may repel the other. Such is the powerful influence of colour on the mind and on our emotions. But basically, each colour has got its own domain that is, each colour affects us differently.

The astrologers have also identified the planets each one with a certain colour. Again the numerologists have also categorised the colours with particular numbers. Below you will find some amazing combinations:-

Number		**Colour**
1	=	Black.
2	=	Yellow.
3	=	Purple.
4	=	Orange.
5	=	Blue.
6	=	Green.
7	=	Grey.
8	=	Brown.
9	=	Red.

Planets and metals are also linked by the astrologers in some such ways that are listed below:-

Gold is the metal representing the sun and silver for the moon. Other colours were given to other planets such as red to Mars, green or light blue to Venus, dark blue or purple to Jupiter, black or brown to Saturn and variable colours to Mercury. Thus the sun and the other planets are linked with the colours by the astrologers.

Exponents of psychic sciences teach us that both, the stars and numbers have a great influence on our daily lives. The influence of colours combined with the power of the stars and the forces of numbers have a tremendous impact on our bodies.

Astrologers have also sorted out and linked some gem stones to the days of the week and the month, we are born in. A few examples will elucidate this. Sunday (*Sun*) is for gold and yellow gems;

Day	Planets		Gems
Monday	(Moon)	for	pearls and white stones;
Tuesday	(Mars)	for	blood rubies;
Wednesday	(Mercury)	for	turquoise, sapphire;
Thursday	(Jupiter)	for	amethyst, purple stones;
Friday	(Venus)	for	emerald and green stones;
Saturday	(Saturn)	for	white diamond or onyx.

Having known the relation of the colours and numbers with the planets and gems, have we gained any knowledge regarding their influence on our bodies? The electromagnetic waves from the colours, the metals and the gems, have all combined to affect our muscular, mental and nervous systems. These have physiological and psychological reactions on us and various fields of operations.

In America, the colour technology was applied in schools, restaurants and hotels and also in hospitals which revealed miraculous effects. In the Coffee bars the blue fluorescent lights were replaced for better sale of Coffee; in hotels salads served in green plates gave double dividends; in schools a combination of black board colours with those of chalks and painting of the interiors with pastel colours, made the lethargic students pick up fast and stop yawning; in hospitals better results were obtained when white walls were repainted with light almond colours in general wards and the recuperating bedrooms were successively painted blue, lavender, yellow and green for added results as the patients went on recovering.

When I was the Secretary of the Safety Committee for 13 years, I implemented many colour combinations in the working shed, in the factory, the canteen and office rooms. It was believed that painting the various machine parts in appropriate colours reduced accidents appreciably. By painting the canteen walls with suitable colour combinations, people felt relaxed and were revitalised for their work again.

In the recess period in the factory, "music" was introduced, which yielded better results.

Now, that we have discussed at length the inter-relations among colours, planets, numbers and gems, we should be convinced how and why these things help us in guiding and curing our diseases. The light comes from a long distance, but the colours present in the light are not distorted, through this long journey. Similarly, the planets all scattered and at various distances, also affect us in various degrees, according to the condition and position of the heavenly bodies and the time and place of our birth. The very fact that the moon influences the high and low tides in the rivers and seas, and also in the menstrual cycles of females as well as in the health of men, we are simply left to wonder how all these really affect our health and our fortune too.

Do not be a fatalist, you can possibly change your health by manipulation of a combination of various devices mentioned.

Hypnosis is another method by which you can imbibe colour into your body and mould it by your will power to cure a disease.

It has been experimented in the U.S.A. and it was found that colours do affect our health and thinking. Sit on yogic pose of Padmasana, relax your mind and body, exhale all the breaths, then inhale and pull up your body and mind, hold your breath for 10 seconds and then concentrate your mind on particular colours at the centre of your forehead. Do this exercise ten times for a week. You will gradually feel that the colour you were concentrating on, will pervade your chest, abdomen, even upto your toes. In the beginning, if you find it difficult to concentrate on a particular colour, then take a colour chart from the market, look at it and then concentrate. I have already told you that for performing a particular type of job or to deal with a particular type of person, you need the help of a particular colour. And this is done the way described.

Have you heard the term Chromotherapy? People, in India are treating diseases by drinking water charged with coloured rays from the sun or massaging such coloured oil on the ailing part of the body for relieving the ache.

(7) Physical Methods

In the early part of this century, pathological and microscopic analysis were successful in locating the cause of organic diseases and thus, to search for a remedy was not difficult. But for depression or mania or for those who suffered from schizophrenia, pathological or microscopic analysis did not help much. People believed that the psychoneurosis or an anxious state of mind was due to weakness of character and lack of moral fibre. Lunatic asylums were full of these patients. At this stage, people like Sigmund Freud came to the rescue. He devised a new method of interpretation and treatment called psychoanalysis which has been discussed earlier in this book.

But it was found that at stages, this procedure also failed to cure depressed persons, when it was discovered that some mental diseases at certain points are due to the chemical changes in the brain.

Thus came to use of psychotrophic drugs. But the side effects told against them. Often, the hypnotic drugs had hangover effects. It was then formulated that the anti-depression drugs may be given in acute cases only and should be gradually tapered off while counselling and psycho-therapy be increased, to bring back the patient to the normal level.

Researchers have discovered that the body manufactures its own animal opiate called *Enkephalin* which keeps us most of the time in a physical and mental equilibrium. When the level of enkephalin drops too low, the miserable depression sets in.

Our body has a big electro-chemical factory. Electrical impulses run to and from our brain to cause and promote chemical changes in the brain. The brain is our computer centre, and in turn this organ sends messages to the glands and tissues. If we can keep our mental balance, all the time, then the pituitary gland (the master gland) will activate properly and positive emotions will flow. When, even with the best efforts, we fail to maintain the balance of our brain, we can fall back on physical medicines. Some of the main types of drugs are

(a) *Tryclicic Group Therapy.*

(b) *Mono-Amineoxydase Group (*MAO*) Therapy.*

(c) *Lithium Carbonate Therapy.*

All these groups of medicines have many side effects and any physician using these drugs should be very cautious.

For example, in the Tryclicic Group, the *Tofranil* or *Triptizol* has many side effects in the course of 3 to 6 months treatment (that the patients have to undergo), such as dry mouth, blurring of eyes, upset bladder function and feeling sleepy all the time. Another effect noticed is that the patient may undergo a *Mood Swing*. However, this *Mood Swing*, which is very dangerous, is otherwise also very common in many *Depressed Patients*.

Among the M.A.O. group of medicines, *Ipronizid* changes the depressed person into a hypermaniac when he becomes over active.

These medicines act better if the patients' phobic symptoms such as fear of open spaces or over crowding is there. But even such good medicines have got adverse side effects, such as liver damage and bad headaches. For these medicines, the patient should also follow the list of forbidden foods. Now, there are better drugs like tetracyclics that have entered the market.

Lithium Carbonate is another drug invented by an Australian Scientist. Lithium Carbonate is prescribed for patients suffering from Primary Endogenous Depression (P.E.D.) and hypermania (mania to overwork). This drug not only rapidly settles the maniac excitement, but it can also prevent attacks from re-occurring. The difficulty is that as this drug is generally prescribed for a long time, continuous blood toxicity level is to be monitored. The danger is that if an overdose is put in, signs of toxicity are seen and tremour of hands and raging thrust is the result.

Many common mild low mood syndromes are due to diets deficient in Vitamins B and C, specially Vitamin B Complex.

Due to the shortage of Vitamin B_1 (Thiamin), depression, irritability, failure to concentrate and defective memory are noticed. All these constitute Endogenous Depression (E.D.). Shortage of Vitamin B_3 (Nicotinic Acid), B_6 (Pyrodoxine), B_{12} (Cynocobalamine) and C (Ascorbic Acid) can produce low moods and wretchedness. Deficiency in Vitamin B_{12} only induces pernicious anaemia (P.A.). For loss of appetite and insomnia, Vitamin B_{12} taken for a length of time, works miracles.

For patients who do not want to visit the doctor frequently, but suffer from depression, or are hypermaniac, or suffer from loss of appetite or insomnia, can try B complex combined with Vitamin C for a few months and observe the results.

Many people medicate themselves with tranquilisers like Librium or Valium to ward off their insomnia or depression. But they are warned that these tranquilisers may provide temporary relief. But eventually patients could become addicts.

In the case of Mrs. R. Chakravorty, she was told by the doctor, to take two tablets of *Campose* everyday to cure her insomnia and anxiety, as if she could not survive without those. But since I took up the case, I asked her why she wanted to fight with the shadow? As, I told her, since she was quite free from danger, why should she continue with the sedatives? Thus, she reduced the dose from two tablets a day to 1 tablet in two days and gradually in a few weeks she dropped the sedative altogether.

Tranquilisers may make the patient feel more comfortable, but they do not solve the basic problem, which is causing the distress, is not diagnosed properly, and left only on the tranquilisers or sedatives, the illness may take a serious turn. If at all, the tranquilisers are to be taken, they should not be continued for more than a week or so and in the meantimes, proper investigation should be started for identifying the cause of the disease.

As a last resort for depressed patients, the E.C.T. (Electroplexy or rather *Electro-Convulsive-Therapy*) is tried. The E.C.T. was invented by two Italian psychiatrists in the 1930s. This therapy can alter the mood of a patient rapidly and drastically. Generally, it is given to *Hypermaniac* patients to control over-activity. Previously, the process used to be very unpleasant and painful. But, these days, it is as simple as to give a prick and an electric shock into a small vein on the back of the hand and the patient drops off to sleep. Later, the patient may have a slight headache and some temporary loss of memory. Now that Chemotherapy has been introduced, E.C.T. is losing popularity fast. Of course, in some acute or imminent cases, E.C.T. shows very quick results compared with other chemical methods of treatment.

All general physicians (G.P.) should to some extent, be therapists as well as psychiatrists. The cause of the ailment cannot always be detected by chemical, microscopic and other instrumental devices alone. The best method to treat a patient, is to allow him to express his or her troubles or discomforts. Sometimes they mention Vague symptoms, which may be irrelevant to the physician. It is the duty of the physician whether he be a G.P. or a psychiatrist, to allow the patient to describe his ailments, if he is in a position to do so. This facilitates the therapist to proceed in a right direction. This is really an art in dealing with patient's fear and anxiety.

CHAPTER VIII

Looking Back

Now you have known what our Soma (body) and Psyche (mind) are meant for. You have also known that human being is the most intelligent living organism who can think and develop, for his betterment and also for those that live with him.

You have seen that happiness, which is our ultimate goal, can be achieved by love. By generating love within, we can evade many somatic diseases.

If you are sincere to yourself, you can be sincere to others also. This can be achieved by trust in God. You cannot just evade God. You may choose to call it God or Nature. But when you close your eyes and start meditating, you will feel that you are placed in a beautiful surrounding, soothing environs. This is God.

I felt it when I used to sit in the softly green-lit surroundings in the meditation hall at the Vivekananda Rock Temple at Kanya Kumari. I also used to feel it when I used to sit in seclusion for hours on the rocks, facing the snowy peaks of the Himalayas at Chandanwari near Pahelgaon in Kashmir.

But if you don't want to travel such long distances and want to enjoy the peace of mind and have a tranquil ensemble all around, you should meditate at a quiet place early in the morning, in or around your premises.

But by peace of mind alone, you cannot possibly live a disease-free life! For that, you have to develop some correct food habits and follow some routine of simple Yogic Exercises. Your behaviour towards yourself and others, including the opposite sex, counts a lot in building a healthy body and a healthy mind.

A lot has been said here as to what methods are to be adopted by different categories of persons at different ages. A quick resume may help.

I have indicated earlier that there are three critical phases in our life, viz: at the age of 20, 35 and 60.

The age at 20 is the sunset of adolescence and sunrise of youth. At the age of 35 onwards, the mental acumen starts dwindling and at the age of 60, man starts feeling that he is losing all the treasure for ever.

It has been found that most of the great men showed their colour during the age of 18 and 28. It has also been seen that most of the crimes are committed during this period. In order to tread this path in a right way, one should mobilize enough courage to follow the well-laid track of restraint and forbearance as regards food, thought and activities.

When an young man crosses the threshold of 20, he is to inculcate the habit of taking simpler food, and more fruits and vegetables. He should also start shedding some courses of non-vegetarian food. In his daily diet, he should include some sprouted nuts (whole) and cereals. Yoghurt (Dahi), Gur and Dates, Citrus and other juicy fruits (Nimboo etc.) and plenty of water (four to six glasses) are also necessary.

To maintain body heat and energy, we need carbon. This carbon is abundant in Jawar, Bajra, Dates, Gur, Plantain (Kela) etc. The growing body also needs nitrogen which is found in milk products and pulses (Dal).

Iron is needed more for women (15 gms. per day) than for men (10 gms. per day), especially for those beyond 20. Among many other things, this iron is abundant in onion, raddish, turnip (Salgam) soyabean, karela, green plantain (Kela), papaya (Papita) etc.

When you cross 20, generally you face the outside world and get infected through the environment and food. To combat these infections, you need chlorine, which is available in coconuts, dates, tomato, plantain, cabbage and many green vegetables.

At this age, men and women worry for their tooth, skin, complexion and hair. These are taken care of by silicon, available in all juicy fruits, raddish and cabbage, etc.

The importance of iodine is known to most of us. The deficiency of iodine in the Thyroxine secreted by the Thyroid gland, causes stunted growth. Mothers deficient in this item may give birth to physically or mentally deficient babies or may not give birth to a child at all. Excess iodine, on the other hand, may cause goitre. Onion, pineapple, many sour fruits, dhania, zeera, kali mirch as well as ginger contain this iodine.

Whatever may be the pressure of his studies or work for his livelihood after 20, the youngman must sleep for 7 to 8 hours every day and must also have complete rest for fifteen minutes after every 2 hours of hard labour during the course of his work. That is what Napolean and Churchill did. He should try to leave his bed at least half an hour before sunrise and meditate on the bed itself after gulping two glasses of water. He should do some Yoga Asanas like Pavan Muktasan, Padmasan and finally Shavasan for some time. At this age, he should practise Bhujangasan twenty times, twice daily, in the early morning to keep his spine healthy.

After clearing his bowels, he should come out in the open air, do some Surya Pranam, Sirsasan and Pranayam. For Sirsasan, he should be sure that he is not suffering from such serious diseases like blood pressure, heart ailments etc. or other abdominal diseases.

In the afternoon he should indulge in some outdoor games, at least for half an hour daily, which will make him perspire. In the evening, he should take out some time to study religious books to keep control over his mind, at least for half an hour everyday.

At night before going to bed, he should carry out Matsendrasan and Gomukhasan and finally after sitting in the posture of Vajrasan, he should lie on his left and have deep sleep.

Matsendrasan and Gomukhasan will also make his spine supple and guard him from sexual pitfalls and boost his nervous system also.

When he reaches the age of 30, his life style gets altered. Most people get married near about this age. Till now, he was thinking of and working for his studies and for establishing himself as a worthy citizen. He was busy in building his body and health and also knowledge. After this age, he is burdened with an extra responsibility of dealing with his wife and sharing lot of time and attention and energy with her. Many people think that in a married life, man loses much of his precious vital force. This is not so, if it is not misused.

As a matter of fact, the semen ejaculated is regularly reproduced in routine, unless the same is abnormally exhausted. The male sperm cells and the fluid vehicle are secreted by the testes and the prostrate gland respectively in a regular routine, unless the process is impaired by some defect or disease. Sex, once or twice a week is justified for the newly married couple, but gradually it should be modulated to once or twice a fortnight, and later it should be still further reduced to once a month till, the wife reaches the stage of menopause.

Sex is not intercourse or ejaculation only, it is basically the orgasm, the height, that matters. To be able to culminate in orgasm is an art. This can also be achieved at a later stage of life by good relations with the spouse, exchange of looks and smiles, having amusing jokes and hearty laughs by tender strokes and hugs and ultimately by making love.

The period from the age of 30 to 40 is a very precious one. At the beginning of this period, one is supposed to be at the pinnacle of one's wisdom, but after some time, there is a drooping down, especially from the age of 35, unless efforts are made to keep oneself boosted up.

This is the time when one falls victim to tobacco and alcohal. At this time, parents and the education centres have already laid off their hands and wife is only a new associate who cannot influence one much. The colourful affluence all around, including the so-called friends, can seduce one to the dingy blind lane of no return.

Hence to be safe from the pitfalls, one should regularly read good literature, at least for half an hour daily for six days a week, and keep another half an hour reserved in the morning and half an hour in the later part of the day for Yogic Exercises.

As one progresses beyond the age of thirty, one is to take special care of the spine and body formation and sustenance of youth. One should carry on with Matsendrasan and Gomukhasan in the evening for achieving this goal. These asanas also keep guard against sexual anomalies. Dhanurasan and Ustrasan will also keep one's spine healthy. If one is not suffering from any heart disease, one should also practise Sarvangasan which can withstand practically all the common diseases.

When one crosses 35, one has to be sure that one has started entering old age, physically and mentally. To keep fit sexually and otherwise, one should inculcate the habit of some special Yogic Exercises like Mahabandha Mudra, Mulabandha Mudra and either or both of Mahamudra and Mahabedha.

Mahabandha regulates the gonads or the sex glands (Testes in men and Ovaries in women) and keeps the body free from sex irregularities. Mulabandha helps retrieve the impairment of the kidneys, testes, prostrate gland in men and ovary in women.

The exercises like Mahamudra and Mahabedha have some process common for practising them. For these, one is to squeeze the anus and the abdomen alongwith the control of his breadth. These are beneficial for controlling indigestion and constipation and also for guarding against piles etc. These exercises regulate the sexual urge and the flow of semen in men.

If one has taken good care of various aspects in the period prior to 60, one has nothing to worry about. As the pattern of physical, sexual and mental activities suddenly change, many people suffer from depression, culminating in physical and mental diseases. After 60, one should switch over to long morning walks and engage oneself in creative hobbies, apart from undertaking yogic exercises and other activities mentioned for the earlier periods of life.

Food regulation as well as physical and mental exercises at this stage are must, to enable one to keep fit.

For the morning breakfast, if one can afford, one should alter the food habits. Some fruit juice and sprouted nuts and cereals are suggested. Lunch should include Yoghurt (Curd), Dal, some green vegetables and some roots, along with a few chapatis and a full big glass of water after half an hour of lunch. At this period of life, a full glass of pure water after every two - three hours is a must. This will keep the skin and bowels healthy.

A word or two regarding food habits at this point of life. Apart from the minerals, the body would need six essential components in graded amounts i.e. Proteins, Carbohydrates, Fats, Salt, Vitamins and Water.

Proteins help body-building, generate body heat, produce anti-bodies as well as juices like Pepsin, Tripsin etc. which are required for metabolism, - the digestive programmer. In the human body, one can store carbohydrate and fats, but not proteins. After the age of 25, the protein requirements of the body decreases from 85 to 65 gms. per day for men, and from 75 to 50 gms. per day for women. Excess protein after 25 or 30 is redundant for the body and is liable to cause various diseases including Cancer.

Carbohydrates are basically a fuel element. They also help produce Vitamin 'B' and 'K' in the intestines and help avoid constipation.

Fats act as a body energy reservoir. They can dissolve Vitamin 'A' 'D', 'E' and 'K' and make them suitable for the body. They prevent skin diseases and constipation.

Salt, either Sodium Chloride or any other salt, is present to the extent of 4% of the body. Its deficiency will make the body sick.

Vitamins 'A', 'B', 'C', 'D', 'E', 'K', and 'P' and Nicotinic Acid are also required by the body, though in a meagre quantity, but are very essential for our well-being.

Pure water has got various uses. It helps digestion, keeps the skin healthy and prevents constipation among various other functions. An adult should drink at least 6 to 8 glasses of water in summer and four to six glasses in the winter to keep fit.

At and after the age of 60, active participation in sex is to be regulated to a minimum or gradually tapered down and the mental and physical activities are to be enhanced. One is to keep one's Libido excited in different ways.

To activate one's Libido, one has to inculcate the habit of creative work, like gardening, singing or playing musical instruments, writing, painting (on canvas) or painting and polishing the furniture or toys, sculpturing and the like. But for starting all these, one has to have acquired some interest and thus knowledge for all these activities especially during the period from 40 to 60 or earlier. These creative activities will give him enough tranquility, pleasure and ecstasy.

These strategic periods for women are different from those of men. For men, if these periods are 20, 35 and 60, for women these can be divided at 15, 30, 40 and 60 years of age.

Generally, Indian women start ovulating round the age of 12 and 15. Thereafter, they become capable of bearing a child. From that time onwards, their structure of body starts changing and just before 20, they acquire maximum physical beauty. They grow more egoistic at this age; ego in a broader sense, of course. They are proud of their beauty and they love to be appreciated on all fronts; physical, educational and any other attainment. What is more precarious is that they develop a desire to give vent to their sexual urge after the age of 20.

After 20, it is a very crucial period. Once they get the opportunity to have an orgasm, it is difficult to stop them then onward. So, after the age of 20, if they are married, they are comparatively safe. Otherwise, they should remain deeply engaged in hard labour, or they should be fully engrossed in various activities like studies, religious discourses, outdoor sports, judo, karate, fine art or creative art.

The second threshold of their life is at the age of 30. This is the golden period for women. The best time for them to bear a child is some time between 24 and 34. Sexologist say that it is advisable for women not to give birth to a child after the age of 32-34. Beyond this age, the muscles of the reproductive centre lose much of their elasticity and thus the child birth becomes difficult and painful. The best time to bear a child is very near the age of 30. When a woman bears a child at this age, she is at her physical and mental best. As she gets on to higher age, she starts losing her physical charm, unless she tries to maintain it by proper food and yogic exercises.

Women, in general, are destined to become mothers unless family circumstances or physical ailments prevent them from doing so.

From the very age of 15, she should start taking food, abundant in protein and iron. From the age of 20 onward, she should be selective for food containing Vitamin 'A', 'B' and 'K'. Again at and around 30, she should be particular in maintaining Vitamin 'C' and calcium in her food, apart from taking enough iron during pregnancy and lactation.

As far as yoga exercises are concerned, they are mostly common with men. But women may perform some of the easy Asanas except the Mudras during pregnancy and three months after the child birth. And for five days or so in a month, generally from the age of 12 to 45, they should refrain from any type of exercises.

The next threshold period for women is the age of 40. Near about this age, there is a hormone change in them. Nature warns them that it is time they should realise that they can no longer bear a child. Menopause occurs any time between 40 and 50. For most of the Indian women, it happens approximately by the age of 44 and 46.

Due to the change in hormone, women lose much of their beauty and most of them become bulky and disproportionate. At this change-over period, their sexual urge once shoots up and then has an ugly fall. They lose response to sex and also lose much of their physical beauty. This is a precarious period for them.

During the period between 30 and 40, women should be very particular about selecting yoga exercises and should have food of specific nature containing Vitamin B_2 and B_{12} for controlling their sex urge and general health. They should stop eating non-vegetarian food and take more of Gur and Dates, replacing sugar. Other food items are mostly similar to those for men from the age of 50 to 60.

They should, at this age, switch over more to household activities likes stitching, knitting, teaching young people and taking up social activities. This will be beneficial for maintaining their physical beauty and mental health.

The practice of restricted diet for Indian widows also holds good for women between the age of 45 - 60, due to the hormonal change in them. In olden days, women at and after the age of 60, would travel to religious shrines and when at home, involve themselves in religious activities. Of many reasons for this, the prime one was to divert the sexual urge repressed in them.

After 60, men also want to give vent to their sexual urge, but the case for men is slightly different from that of women. As men are extrovert in general, they can get a relief by artistic, literary or cultural activities. In an Indian environment, the excess, if any, is accepted and absorbed by the society. In case the society does not accept it, they may also like women, turn lunatic or lewd. Hence, for men, as well as for women, when they cross the age of 60, it is better for them to get involved in religious discourses and meditate on the cosmic phenomenon.

CHAPTER IX

Happiness is the Key to Success

We have seen that all we want is wealth and happiness. But to achieve these, physical and mental health is a must.

Happiness, is a treasure of the mind and wealth is a treasure of the material world. Both these are indispensable for us. But how do we acquire these two diverse factors?

In the last few chapters, it is told that we must have good health first and then only can we work hard to acquire wealth.

If we don't neglect health rules adversely, we don't generally have impaired health. But often, it is seen that our mind is affected by outside circumstances or some inner thought without our conscious knowledge.

Some messages are registered in the brain even before the baby is actually born. Then, upto the age of five, is a very susceptible period for the child, and the mother is responsible for it. From the age of 5 to 10, father stealthily comes into the picture. This influence gradually increases along with other environmental influences. From the age of 10 to 20, the child registers various feelings like, love, hate, magnanimity, jealousy and other emotions. The age of 20 to 35, is very important, as during that period various socio-commercial events are registered by the young man. It is said that the period from 18 to 28 is a crucial period, when a genius or a scoundrel takes shape. From the age of 32 to 35, is the period of his efficiency and ideas are confirmed and he is supposed to be a fully mature person. After the age of 35, physical and mental decay starts and then we should be careful to ward it off. From the age of 35 to 38, the drooping curve is not steep, but thereafter, it declines at a faster rate. Regarding old age, much has been said in the last chapter. But here I want to impress you regarding the contribution of the parents to the child.

Of all these, from the fertilisation of the embryo upto the age of 5 is very important for recording and recall.

Dr. Wilder Penfield, a Neuro-Surgeon from McGill University in Montreal in 1951, began to produce exciting evidence to confirm and modify theoretical concepts, as to why some memories are available more for recall than others.

For these recordings mostly the mother and the father are very important. Thereafter, when the child goes to school or is exposed to the outside world, he is bombarded by outside concussions. The furrows thus produced in the brain are deep and the memories are not forgotten easily. They may take bad shapes if and when various other wrong or negative experiences are compounded with these.

The nine months in the womb is very important. The mother's behaviour and her psychology are very important in that period. She has to play a very important role upto that time when the baby is five. She has to provide maximum body contact and stroke the child which would provide the infant with a psychology of "I am O.K. and you are O.K." This is a psychology that gives a feeling that not only am I good, but the whole world is just as good and pleasant.

Your Behaviour

Behavioural science, is a great subject and is dealt with in details by various research scholars in different institutions. I repeatedly stress that as the mother plays an important role for the bright future of the baby, we are to see that she is groomed very carefully, to enable us to have a mature future generation.

In our modern society, this aspect is gradually losing its importance, as people are getting more and more interested in the material and mechanical ways of life.

When the child grows into adulthood, he starts understanding the various ways of life, and is able to play the game of transaction. As the child enters adulthood, he should be taught the art of *Transactional Analysis* (T.A.). You are not to confuse it with the Transcendental Meditation (T.M.), mostly advocated by Maharishi Mahesh Yogi and others, for arousing the *Kundalini* by deep meditation; guiding the course into the Cosmic World.

According to Eric Berne, Transactional Analysis (T.A.) is the method of examining the social intercourse when two or more encounter each other.

Every individual has got 3 states of behaviour in him/her, viz.,

Parent

Adult

Child

A parent is not the combination of father and mother, but it is the attitude that is. Similarly, every individual who comes upto the age of adulthood is not adult but is the attitude that is. Finally, the child in this context, is the attitude and behaviour of the individual.

All of us are playing the Parent, Adult, Child Game (the P.A.C. Game) in every transaction consciously or unconsciously, all the time. But, if we can master the P.A.C. Game profitably, we may achieve peace and prosperity.

THE P.A.C. GAME

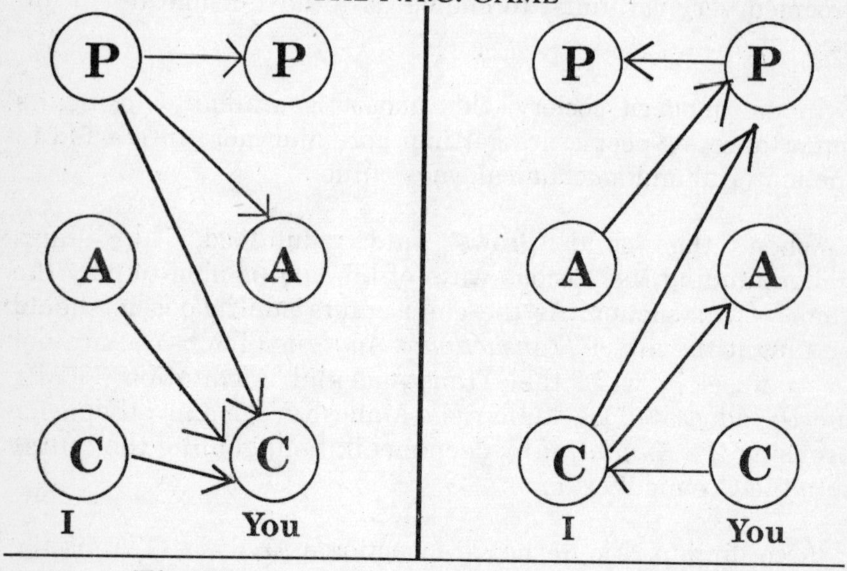

Fig. P

Fig. Q

In the illustration above, and you are confronting each other in two different patterns depicted in Figure P and Q. These are only two sets of games that are illustrated. But you can draw at your leisure and interact in different transaction for different situations, which will be very interesting for you.

These transactions culminate in building good relations and help in developing our personality and it also gives enormous opportunities to solve our day-to-day problems. A mature personality promotes good mature emotions in us and it helps in releasing positive hormones. As was mentioned earlier in this book, these positive hormones help to build up good physical health as well.

The Transactional Analysis (T.A.) spearheads into four possible life positions held with respect to one's own self and others. These are:-

1. I am not O.K. .... You are O.K.
2. I am not O.K. .... You are not O.K.
3. I am O.K. .... You are not O.K.
4. I am O.K. .... You are O.K.

The first stage of the position:-

I am not O.K.- You are O.K. is prevalent in the baby upto the age of 12 months.

The second stage:-

I am not O.K. - You are not O.K. prevails upto the age of 24 months. Then as the child grows he passes through the third stage:-

I am O.K. - You are not O.K. Most of people get stuck at this stage, unless and until someone is mature enough to move on to the fourth stage, that is:-

I am O.K. - You are O.K. To reach this fourth stage, people are to pass through severe turmoil. He is to fight against all his previous recordings, unless they were not erased by further recordings.

This requires more clarifications, for you to understand. To move from the third stage to the fourth, is rather difficult, because most people are so egoistic that they don't accept that there may be anybody better than themselves. At this stage, the candidate is to be put in such an environment that he will start disagreeing with the previous recordings and notions and beliefs. At the same time if he is given further doses of good emotions, then he will not only forget his old ideas and will start developing new ideas, but will be a changed man.

This game of Transactional Analysis (T.A.) can be symbolically represented as shown below:-

I = I
Y = You

√ = OK
× = Not OK

B (3)	I — √ Y — ×	I — √ I — √	**A (4)**
D (1)	I — × I — ×	I — × I — √	**C (2)**

Situation	Disposition	Stage	Quality
(A) I am O.K.	—You are O.K. —	(4)	Most efficient man.
(B) I am O.K.	— You are not O.K. —	(3)	Suspicious man.
(C) I am not O.K.	— You are O.K. —	(2)	Self-Confused man.
(D) I am not O.K.	— You are not O.K. —	(1)	Creates problems for himself.

Having thus known four different pictures of human behaviour, you may play the game of Transactional Analysis (T.A.) also yourself, and try to analyse different personalities including yourself. This is also an interesting game to play.

Generally, people try to change others, with futile results. But, if everyone of us try to change ourselves, the picture of the whole world will change and emerge differently.

The Last Word

Good language, good behaviour and sincere work will lead us to attain peace, pleasure and prosperity.

If we go through the Srimad Bhagwad Geeta, our sacred Indian epic, we will find in:-

(II/38) That "Man of honour should do some deed (Kirti) which will establish (name and) fame without which even death is better." Again, in

(III/14) We find that "*Work* is the seed of all the creation" (and so) in;

(II/48) We should *Work* earnestly without the apprehension of winning or losing". Again in;

(III/37) "Rajo Goona (Over-active quality) leads (us) to lust, which ultimately drives us to *Anger*, which is our acute *Enemy*", (and hence)

(III/26) "Wise men should inspire active (persons) so that they may be induced to *Work*".

Thus, *Work is the only Way to Attain Peace*, which is again told in,

(II/65), "If you attain pleasure (Not by the satisfaction of the senses), you will wipe out sorrows and thus will attain *Eternal Peace*".

We have seen that meditation, love and faith, are all inter-related and one only leads to the other, culminating in absolute ecstasy (excessive joy) and you get inspiration for *Work and Devotion*.

A recent example of Mr. Saparia, a businessman in Bombay, will illustrate this. Both his private and business life changed gradually as he started meditation from 4 O'clock in the morning everyday. Yoga transformed his life and as a result, he started to take problems in his stride, whether the intricate ones at the factory or simpler ones at home. It affected his enviornment so much that the people also changed along with him and there was amity (friendly relations) all around him.

But, what is meditation, at all? In the Bhagwad Geeta, we find, "Through *Meditation*, the *Self* is seen". When we become absolved in the *Self*, by turning our mind from outside to inside (through meditation), we experience *Peace, Courage, Love* and *Strength*. These, in the long run, free us from *Anxiety, Anger* and *Fear* by which we fill our days with *Joy*.

Now, that you have completed all the lessons, prepare yourself to start work.

In the course of the day and night, reserve an hour for meditation in the early mornings, and feel the difference yourself. Start with 15 minutes first, and gradually you will not know how it stretches into longer hours to give you the *Nector of Life*.

So, *Love* and *Pleasure* are the keys to *Happiness,* and *Happiness is the Key to Success.*

BOOKS FOR FURTHER READING

1. Conquest of Happiness — *Bertrand Russell* (1955).
2. Defeating Depression — *Dr. C.A.H. Watts, OBE, MD* (1980).
3. Family Health Guide — *Readers Digest* (1972).
4. How to Live 365 Days in a Year — *Dr. J.A. Schendler, MD* (1962).
5. How your Psychic Powers can Make you Rich — *Davit St. Clair* (1975).
6. Stay Younger - Live Longer — *J.V. Carney* (1976).
7. Therapeutics of Nervous Diseases — *Dr. Charles Porter Hart, MD* (1973).
8. You Don't Have to Ache — *Dr. Arthur A. Michele, MD* (1974).
9. Yoga, Illustrated Dictionary — *Harvey Day* (1974).
10. I am O.K. - You are O.K. — *Thomas, A. Harris - MD* (1974).
11. Yoga, Asans Simplified — *Shri Yogendra* (1959).